ABOVE YPRES

ABOVE YPRES

The German Air Force in Flanders 1914-1918

BERNARD DENECKERE

FireStep
Press

FireStep Press
An imprint of FireStep Publishing

Gemini House
136-140 Old Shoreham Road
Brighton
BN3 7BD

www.firesteppublishing.com

First published in Great Britain by
FireStep Publishing, 2013

© 2013 Bernard Deneckere

ISBN 978-1-908487-30-8

Cover design by Ryan Gearing

Typeset by Graham Hales

Printed and bound in Great Britain

Table of Contents

Preface and Acknowledgements

Like so many concepts of modern warfare, the use of aircraft on a large scale was first developed during the First World War.

Although several types of aircraft were available in 1914, and aerial bombing had been carried out in the colonies shortly before the war, generals didn't properly appreciate their military potential. Considering the flimsy nature of these first planes, this was understandable – most were unable to fly higher then a few thousand feet and their average speed of about 96 km/h/60 mph could be reduced to almost nothing in a strong headwind.

It was eventually the pilots and observers who demonstrated the military potential of the aeroplane to their leaders, and this led to the development of specifically designed fighters, bombers and warplanes. The aeroplane was to become an increasingly significant factor as the five-year conflict wore on.

'Air war above Ypres' recreates that momentous period, showing most specifically how Germany's air force performed during the five gruelling years of battle in Flanders, assessing its infrastructure, aircraft, strategy and tactics, and portraying the extraordinary

German aviators ready for take-off during winter 1918 at Meulebeke airfield (collection Maertens Belgium).

During the First World War the German army made several attempts to conquer the strategic town of Ypres in western Belgium. This German map from 28 October 1917 shows a huge concentration of British kite-balloons defending the town. (Collection Levra, Belgium)

courage of all its flying crews. The names of Frankl, Udet, Voss, Goering and 'The Red Baron' – Manfred von Richthofen – are all well known, but what of the other pilots and observers?

Day after day they flew over the Ypres Salient hoping to encounter and destroy their Allied counterparts. By mid-1917, fighter pilots and crews scrambled into the sky to do battle often as many as three times a day. This book is full of eyewitness accounts, official reports and photographs illustrating these heroic endeavours.

It would never have been possible to get this information on to paper without the help of a lot of people from all over the world with whom I have had correspondence, or the numerous specialised internet forums.

My thanks are due to these people, who were generous not only with their time, but also with their expertise. Several people deserve a special mention for providing most of the photos: Robert Tholl, Rick Duiven and Heinz Nowarra from the USA, Philippe Lagnier in France, Christian Nielebock in Germany, Mike O'Connor in the UK and Wim Martens in Belgium.

I also would like to mention my wife and two sons, who encouraged me during my historical research and my sister-in-law Annick for the translation into English.

Bernard Deneckere
Master of History
deneckere@hotmail.com

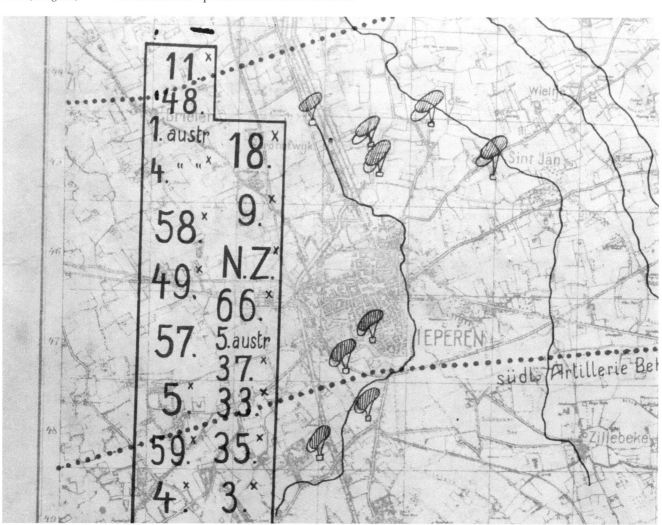

English names of towns and villages	Flemish names
Antwerp	Antwerpen
Bisseghem	Bissegem
Bruges	Brugge
Brussels	Brussel
Cortemarcq	Kortemark
Coucou	Koekuit (a hamlet just outside Menin)
Courtrai	Kortrijk
Coxyde	Koksijde
Cuurne	Kuurne
Dixmude	Diksmuide
Furnes	Veurne
Gheluvelt	Geluveld
Gheluwe	Geluwe
Ghent	Gent
Ghistelles	Gistel
Ghits	Gits
Harlebeke	Harelbeke
Iseghem	Izegem
Menin	Menen
Mouscron	Moeskroen
Neumunster	Nieuwmunster
Nieuport	Nieuwpoort
Ostend	Oostende
Oostcamp	Oostkamp
Passchendaele	Passendale
Poperinghe	Poperinge
Roulers	Roeselare
Thielt	Tielt
Vlisseghem	Vlissegem
Wareghem	Waregem
Wervicq	Wervik
Wevelghem	Wevelgem
Winghene	Wingene
Ypres	Ieper
Zeebruges	Zeebrugge

Glossary of Terms

German Aircraft Types	
Code	**Explanation**
A	Unarmed monoplane, mostly two-seater
B	Unarmed two-seater biplane
C	Armed two-seater biplane
CL	Light C-type, two-seater biplane for low-level attacks against ground troops
D	Armed single-seater biplane
Dr	Armed single-seater triplane
E	Armed single-seater monoplane
G	Twin-engined strategic bomber
GW	Twin-engined seaplane
J	Armed and armoured two-seater biplane for infantry cooperation
R	Giant four-engined strategic bomber-biplane

Flying Squadrons	
Abbreviation/Name	**Unit and translation (German unless otherwise stated)**
AFA	Artillerie Fliegerabteilung – artillery-cooperation squadron
AFP	Armee Flugpark – aviation supply depot
BAO	Brieftaubenabteilung Ostend – Carrier Pigeon Unit Ostend – a strategic bombardment wing
BG	Bombengeschwader – strategic bombardment wing
Bosta	Bombenstaffel – which replaced Kasta from mid-1917
Esc	Escadrille – squadron in the French and Belgian flying forces
FA	Fliegerabteilung – aviation squadron, which replaced the FFA from the end of 1916
FA (A)	Fliegerabteilung (German aviation squadron flying for the artillery)
FFA	Feldflieger-Abteilung – aviation squadron. After the re-organisation of the German flying squadrons in January 1917 forty-eight of these FFAs became FAs
Festungsflieger-Abteilung	Squadron assigned to defend the fortress towns
FLA	Feldluftschiffer-Abteilung – captive balloon unit
FL	Fernlenkboot – a torpedo with an explosive warhead which travelled along the surface of the water, controlled by means of an electric cable
Flandern I	First Flanders armed seaplane squadron (Zeebruges)
Flandern II	Second Flanders armed seaplane squadron (Ostend)

Gruppe	Group
Infanterieflieger	Unit flying contact patrols for the infantry
Jasta	Jagdstaffel – fighter squadron
JG	Jagdgeschwader – permanent wing or group of several Jagdstaffeln
Jg	Jagdgruppe – temporary group of several Jagdstaffeln
Js	Jagdstaffel – fighter (literally 'hunting') squadron
Kagohl	Kampfgeschwader der Obersten Heeresleitung – Bombardment wing of the Army High Command
Kampflugzeug-Abteilung	early name of the fighter squadrons, flying single- and two-engined aircraft
Kasta	Kampfstaffel – bombardment squadron
Kest	Kampfeinsitzerstaffel – single-seater home defence fighter squadron
KG	Kampfgeschwader – strategic bombardment wing
Küsta	Küstenflieger-Abteilung – naval aviation squadron flying for the coastal artillery
MFFA	Marine Feldflieger-Abteilung – naval aviation squadron from the end of 1916
Marinefeldjagdstaffel or Marinejagdstaffel	naval fighter (literally 'hunting') squadron
Marinejagdgeschwader	permanent wing or group of naval squadrons
MLFA	Marinelandflieger-Abteilung – naval aviation squadron until the end of 1916
Schlasta	Schlachtstaffel – specialised ground attack squadron
Schl	Schlasta
Schusta	Schutzstaffel – squadron protecting and escorting reconnaissance aircraft
Seefrosta	Seefrontstaffel – naval squadron protecting the Flemish coast
Rbz	Reichenbildzug – mosaic section with four C-class aircraft equipped with a camera which produced a continuous photographic film
Rfa	Riesenflugzeug-Abteilung – strategic bombardment squadron with four-engined R-type aircraft
Torpedostaffel	naval squadron flying seaplanes armed with torpedoes
Wing	Wings in the RFC and RAF consisted of a number of squadrons.

Formations and Organisations	
Abbreviation	**Full name and translation – German unless otherwise stated**
A	Armee – Army
AK	Armee Korps – Army Corps
AOK	Armee Oberkommando – Army High Command
BEF	British Expeditionary Force
CA	Corps d'Armée – French Army Corps
Grufl	Gruppenführer der Flieger – Officer attached to Corps Headquarters responsible for the aviation squadrons assigned to the Corps
HQ	Headquarters
Kofl	Kommandeur der Flieger – Officer in charge of the aviation squadrons assigned to a German Army
OHL	Obersten Heeresleitung – Army High Command
RAF	Royal Air Force
RFC	Royal Flying Corps
RK	Reserve Korps – Army Reserve Corps
RNAS	Royal Naval Air Service (the air arm of the Royal Navy until 1 April 1918, when it merged with the Royal Flying Corps to form a new service – the Royal Air Force)

Etappen Inspektion – staff officers in charge of army aviation units
Feldflugwesen – field aviation service supplying aircraft, supervising manufacture and building of airfields
Fliegertruppe – the aviation units of the army
Marine Korps Flandern – corps of the German Imperial Navy sent to Flanders
Seeflugwesen – naval aviation service supplying aircraft, supervising manufacture and building of airfields

German Military / Naval / Air Force Ranks	
Bootsmaansmaat	Lower-ranked Petty Officer
Fähnrich zur See	Naval officer candidate
Feldwebel	Sergeant
Flugmaat or Flugmeister	Petty Officer in the naval air service
Flugmeister	
Flugobermaat or Flugobermeister	Chief Petty Officer in the naval air service
Gefreiter	Private 1st Class
Generalleutnant	Lieutenant General
Gruppenführer der Flieger (abb. Grufl)	Chief of the air force of an army group
Inspektor der Fliegertruppen (abb. Idflieg)	Inspector of the German air force
Kapitän	Captain
Kapitänleutnant	Second Lieutenant
Kapitän zur See	Captain (naval)
Kommandeur der Flieger (abb. Kofl)	Officer in charge of aviation squadrons assigned to an army group

Kommandierende General der Luftstreitkräfte (abb. Kogenluft)	Commanding general of the air force
Leutnant	Lieutenant
Leutnant zur See	Lieutnant (naval)
Oberflugmeister	Senior Lieutenant (air force)
Oberleutnant	Senior Lieutenant
Oberleutnant zur See	Senior Lieutenant (naval air service)
Obermaat	Petty Officer (naval air service)
Obermatroos	Private 1st Class (naval air service)
Oberstleutnant	Lieutenant Colonel
Offizier Stellvertreter	Acting officer
Rittmeister	Cavalry Captain
Unteroffizier	Rank below officer
Vizefeldwebel	Sergeant of the Reserve
Vizefeuerwerker	Naval artilleryman of the Reserve

Other Terms

Abbreviation	Explanation
B der Res.	Bayerisch – Bavarian of the Reserve
F	France
FT	Funken Telegraf – German wireless telegraphy
KIA	Killed in action
MIA	Missing in action
PLM	Pour le Mérite. The Kingdom of Prussia's highest military order for German soldiers until the end of World War I
POW	Prisoner of War

CROISEURS ANGLAIS DEVANT OSTENDE

British Marines and aircraft of the RNAS arriving at Ostend on 28 August 1914, as painted by a Belgian refugee (own collection).

1914

The Outbreak of War

By 1910 international tensions divided the major nations of Europe into two potentially hostile camps, with Germany in one and France and Russia in the other. The assassination of Archduke Franz Ferdinand of Austro-Hungary in Sarajevo by Serbian nationalist Gavrilo Princip on 28 June 1914 triggered a chain of threats and ultimatums, which finally resulted in the declaration of war between the two alliances.

Geographically, Germany was situated between its two enemies, France and Russia, so the German military command faced a major tactical problem – wherever they launched an attack, they would immediately be confronted by two enemies simultaneously – one on the east and one on the west border. To avoid this situation the Germans created the Moltke Plan.

The Moltke Plan depended essentially on speed and timing. The Germans had calculated that it would take six weeks for the Russians to mobilise their army, however, mobilisation in Germany and France would take no longer than two weeks. Therefore Germany would throw her major forces into a rapid action against France, calculating that victory could be gained within 39 days. Once the French were defeated on the Western Front, Germany could take on the still-mobilising Russia.

To avoid the well-fortified Franco-German border, the German High Command planned a quick move through Belgium and south to Paris, knocking out the French Army in an attack from behind.

Tension mounted as France mobilised and its armies were made ready. On 2 August 1914 the German Army crossed the border with Luxembourg, and two days later, began the invasion of Belgium. Previously uninvolved in the conflict, Britain could no longer stay on the sidelines, and declared war on Germany on 4 August. The First World War had begun.

German forces gained victory over the Russians with unexpected speed, so temporarily eliminating the threat on the Eastern Front, however, to the west, the Moltke Plan was going wrong. On 8-9 September the French Army and the hastily mobilised British Expeditionary Force successfully held up German forces at the River Marne, forcing them to withdraw and face the French in the Battle of the Aisne, (13-14 September), where they managed to stand their ground.

Two German Zeppelins – the Sachsen and the Z IX – raided Antwerp and the Belgian coast from 25 August until the end of September 1914, as they searched for the British who were advancing through northern France (own collection).

Both sides now tried to break through in the area between Paris and the North Sea, but all these attempts failed, and little by little the front line moved northwards. On 16 October both armies reached the River Lys on the Franco-Belgian border. To the north the small Belgian Army had resisted the German invaders at Antwerp for more than a month, but as Germany launched a major assault, the Belgians finally had to leave their stronghold and withdraw to the west, where the French High Command ordered them to take and hold an area around the River Yser. Four days later the Germans stormed their positions, and part of a German division managed to cross the river, forcing the exhausted Belgian Army to take refuge behind the Nieuport-Dixmude railway. French reinforcements closed the gap, but the situation remained very dangerous until the Belgians flooded the west bank of the River Yser, so preventing all German progress in that area.

Now the only remaining gap in the front line was between the rivers Lys and the Yser, the central point of which was the city of Ypres. The First Battle of Ypres started on 20 October 1914, and wave after wave of German troops stormed the French and British positions. Although all Allied lines were broken, the Germans failed to capture Ypres by the end of the battle on 15 November.

By the end of 1914 the Western Front was established from the North Sea to the Swiss border – a new kind of static warfare with trenches and barbed wire was born.

The German Air Force and the Invasion of Belgium

On 4 August 1914 four German armies were ready to invade Belgium, with air support as follows:

Army Corps	Flying unit	Airfield
First Army	FFA 12 FLA 1	Jülich-Grevenbroich
II AK	FFA 30	Rheydt
III AK	FFA 7	Elsdorf
IV AK	FFA 9	Aachen-Forst
Etappen-Inspekt.* 1	Etappen Flugzeug Park 1	Düsseldorf
Second Army	FFA 23 FLA 2	Höfen Aachen
Guards Corps	FFA 1	Thirimont
VII AK	FFA 18	Eupen
IX AK	FFA 11	Aachen-Brand
X AK	FFA 21	Call
Etappen-Inspekt. 2	Etappen Flugzeug Park 2	Hangelar
Third Army	FFA 22 FLA 7	St-Vith Niederprüm
XI AK	FFA 28	Wallerode
XII AK	FFA 29	Ober-Beslingen
XIX AK	FFA 24	Neuerburg
Etappen-Inspekt. 3	Etappen Flugzeug Park 3	Niedermending
Fourth Army	FFA 6 FLA 3	Trier-Euren Trier
VI AK	FFA 13	Dillingen
VIII AK	FFA 10	Trier-Euren
XVIII AK	FFA 27	Conz
Etappen-Inspekt. 4	Etappen Flugzeug Park 4	Trier
* The Etappen Inspektion groups were army staff officers who were in charge of the army's flying units.		

Every Feldflieger-Abteilung (flying squadron) or FFA had a strength – on paper – of six aeroplanes, approximately half of which were monoplanes (the Taube and Fokker A models). These were A-type aircraft with only one pair of wings, while the other half were B-type – biplanes with two pairs of wings. Significantly at this time, none of these aircraft was armed

FFA 9 was the first unit to go into action, crossing the Belgian-German border together with the first troops. For seven days it was the only FFA supporting the First, Second and Third German Armies. The squadron carried out reconnaissance flights over the fortifications of Liège and searched for Belgian counter-attacks in the region of Tongeren and Sint-Truiden en Waremme. On the first day the aircraft dropped pamphlets over Liège ordering the Belgians to surrender, and dropped a couple of bombs on the city. From 9 August onwards FFA 9 made more extensive forays, flying over the fortifications of Namur, then two days later FFAs 1, 11, 18 and 21 joined the action. Reconnaissance showed that most of the bridges across the River Meuse had been destroyed – on

these forays they also took photos covering the fortifications around Chaudfontaine, Flémalle near Liège and Anday near Namur, producing the first aerial images of the war.

Compelled by the German invasion of Belgium to declare war, Britain mobilised quickly and by 8 August the British Expeditionary Force had landed at the French harbour of Boulogne. This was a serious threat to Germany's planned rapid advance through Belgium, so from 19 August onwards, German pilots were sent out to report back on the movement of British troops, and these were the first German planes to reach the Belgian coast. On 19 August Leutnant Hans Hesse of FFA 12, flew a reconnaissance mission over Namur, Ostend and Bruges, but ran out of fuel. He had to make a forced landing just across the Dutch border near Oostburg, where he was captured by the Dutch. The next day FFA 12 sent another plane over Ghent, Bruges and Ostend and a crew from FFA 21 made a reconnaissance flight of 380 km/ 236 miles to the Belgian coast.

On 22 August a crew from FFA 30 carried out a reconnaissance flight over Courtrai, Audenaerde and Lille in France. All patrols

The men of Feldflieger-Abteilung 6 at Trier, before departing for the front. The unit served in Flanders from the end of October 1914 (own collection).

The remains of a crashed LVG B1 shot down by the French near Bertrix in the Belgian Ardennes on 22th August. The pilot, Leutnant Jansson died, although observer Oberleutnant Stietencron managed to escape (collection Lagnier France).

reported the same thing – they did not find the British, but were able to confirm that the Belgians were retreating in the direction of the fortifications around Antwerp.

Every day the flying units moved to another landing place close behind the advancing armies, so by 24 August the flying units supporting the First Army were on following airfields:

FFA 7	Ghlin	Taubes and Albatros biplanes
FFA 9	Ath	Hansa Taubes
FFA 11	Mons	LVG biplanes
FFA 12	Mons	Albatros monoplanes and biplanes
FFA 30	Peruwelz	AEG biplanes

Between 20 and 30 August, German forces defeated the French Fifth Army at the Battle of Charleroi, and then during the Battle of Mons, 23-24 August, German troops managed to drive back the British, so clearing their way through Belgium. The German Armies now headed for France, leaving only a small corps of reserve troops to fight the Belgian Army in Antwerp. This corps was allocated the newly-created FFA 38, which was formed on 31 August from Festungsflieger-Abteilung 3 (these were aviation units allocated to Germany's major fortress towns), which had been flying from Cologne and Liège. The five monoplanes of the new unit were transferred to an airfield at Sint-Agatha-Berchem, to the north-west of Brussels.

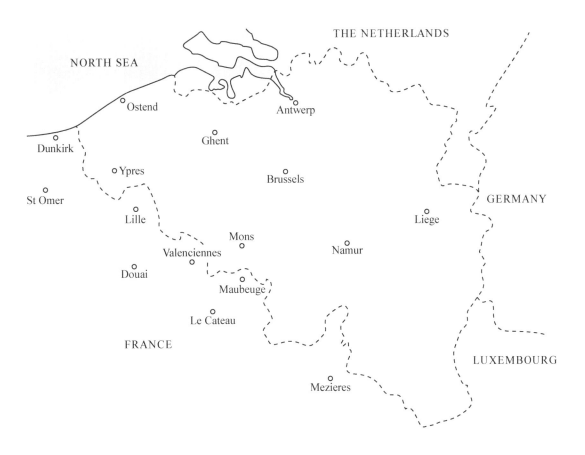

THE NETHERLANDS

NORTH SEA

Ostend

Antwerp

Dunkirk

Ghent

Ypres

Brussels

GERMANY

St Omer

Lille

Liege

Mons

Namur

Valenciennes

Douai

Maubeuge

Le Cateau

FRANCE

LUXEMBOURG

Mezieres

The Air War in Flanders

During the first months of the war, holding Belgium was of lesser importance to the German command, but after the German defeat at the Aisne, both the Allies and Germany launched attacks towards the North Sea in an attempt to get behind the enemy advance. German cavalry and aeroplanes were sent to the north to observe Allied movements, paying particular attention to trains and railways – only by rail could large numbers of troops be transported to make a quick breakthrough.

Another German priority was to capture the ports of Calais, Dunkirk and Boulogne to prevent British reinforcements being shipped in, so a new Fourth Army was formed, composed of four reserve corps, with air support from two FFAs based at Sint-Agatha-Berchem near Brussels: FFA 6 with six Aviatiks flying for the Army Command, and FFA 38, with eight Gotha Tauben, flying for III Reserve Corps.

In mid-October, the new Fourth Army made a breakthrough towards the Belgian coast and on 12 October FFA 38 moved to an airfield at Sint-Denijs Westrem near Ghent, leaving FFA 6 at Sint-Agatha-Berchem. The next day an aircraft of FFA 6 dropped a bomb on Bruges, causing widespread panic

An Albatros B at Namur, August 1914 (Collection Plane).

among the population, but on 14 October a plane of FFA 38 flown by Leutnant Richard Siebel and observer Oberleutnant Günther von Heine, was shot down over Ypres. Wing Commander C R Samson, commander of the aeroplane squadron of the RNAS, was an eye-witness:

> On the way we saw a German monoplane coming along at about 2,000 feet altitude – evidently the Germans were ignorant that the English had arrived at Ypres, as otherwise they wouldn't have been so low. Whilst waiting for it to come over us, we fired at it with the machine-gun and our rifles.
>
> The aeroplane suddenly had its nose down, glided down, evidently hit; jumping into the car, we dashed off in the direction it was taking.
>
> We were somewhat delayed by getting into a cul-de-sac and having to go by a roundabout road, but eventually we found it in a ploughed field. General Montgomery and several soldiers, mostly headquarters clerks, were already on the scene.
>
> The monoplane, a DFW, was practically undamaged, and had only one bullet-hole in it. Research could produce no reason for its descent, as the controls and engine were in working order.
>
> We thoroughly searched the wood, but found no signs of the Germans. I left Osmond with a couple of men to remove the engine, which was a new Mercedes. I sent it to England next day, as it might be of value to our Air Department, being of the very latest type. Osmond burnt the aeroplane, as it was of no use to us.
>
> Late that night the German pilot and his observer were caught by a mounted Belgian gendarme, and brought into Ypres. I attended their examination, which was carried out by the Provost Marshal. They were a very woebegone pair, and quite the opposite of what one expected German aviators to be. They were both terribly scared, and were only too willing to say anything. On arriving at HQ, I found that everybody claimed to have brought the Taube down, including Sir Henry Rawlinson, who had seized my brother's rifle, and fired five shots at it with the cut-out closed. The only man who couldn't claim it was the anti-aircraft pom-pom captain, who was in a fearful rage because he had failed to get his gun into action, through being obstructed by the crowd of generals, etc, all shooting at the Hun. The total bag was counted up to be one Hun aeroplane, five sparrows, three windows, and most of the telegraph-wires in the main square.

Two days later, facing fierce Allied opposition on the Yser front, FFA 38 based at Ghent deployed two Taubes to a forward airfield near the lighthouse at Ostend, charged with locating the French and Belgian positions behind the river Yser.

It was not until the end of October that new squadrons were brought in to reinforce the Fourth Army: FFA 40, based at Handzame, flew for XXIII Reserve Corps in the Boezinge and Dixmude area, and FFA 41, based at Staden made reconnaissance flights between Langemark and Zonnebeke in support of XXVI Reserve Corps. In the meantime, FFA 6 moved to Rumbeke, near Roulers, and became an *Armeeflieger* – a unit assigned to the Army HQ. Supporting the Fourth Army, they were responsible for the whole front line for the Fourth Army. FFA

Planes and airships of the British RNAS near Ostend lighthouse. From late August until the end of October 1914 this little Eastchurch squadron under the command of Charles R Samson operated in Flanders in support of the British marines. No 50 is a Royal Aircraft Factory BE2a – Samson's aircraft of choice (Collection Plane).

38 at Ghistelles became the Fourth Army's second army flying unit.

FFAs 40 and 41 were newly formed units and therefore still had much to learn before they could play any significant role in the air war. On 1 November FFA 41 lost a plane near St-Omer due to the pilot's lack of experience. Disorientated, the crew crossed the lines until a British plane forced them to land deep inside French territory. The two crewmembers, pilot Oberleutnant Hans Lungershausen and observer Leutnant der Reserve Ernst Lengeling, tried to escape but were shot by French territorial troops. Their unit had only moved from Ghent to their forward airfield in Staden the previous day, during which transfer all the pilots lost their way and had to made emergency landings at other airfields.

These FFAs flew the Fokker monoplane, an underpowered aircraft not well suited to reconnaissance or bombing duties.

Observer Hermann Köhl of Feldflieger-Abteilung 41 described their first flights:

During 1914 we flew Fokker two-seaters. These light aircraft struggled to carry the 50 to 100 steel arrows, and throwing these missiles was also very difficult. We wrapped them in a bandolier that we carried under our seat, and which we would unroll above the target. I think we failed to hit the targets due to the fact that we could not aim. By the end of 1914 we carried Fliegermäuschen [little bats] on board – these were a type of grenade with a large fin to make it fall on its head.

To the south, the German Sixth Army had reached the River Lys and crossed the

Gotha LE3 Taube of Feldflieger-Abteilung 38 at the Ferme Zomerloos in Ghistelles on 8 November 1914. Engine: 100 hp Mercedes DI; wingspan: 14.5 m /47 ft 7 in; length: 10 m/32 ft 9 in; loaded weight: 1,026 kg/2,257 lb; maximum speed: 96 km/h/60 mph (Collection Plane).

Belgian border at Menin and Wervicq. On 12 October aircraft of FFA 4 took off for their first patrols above Flanders in support of XIII Army Corps.

One of these pioneering crews, Oberleutnant Sperrle and pilot Schöller, made a morning flight from their airfield at Valenciennes, exploring the region around Courtrai and Tournai, strategically important for their railway yards. Then in the late afternoon Oberleutnant Sperrle and civil pilot Stetten revisited the same places. The next morning Stetten and Oberleutnant Nuber made a trip to the coast, surveying Wervicq, Ypres , Furnes, Nieuport, Dixmude, Roulers, Iseghem, Courtrai and Tournai – but failed to find any enemy movements.

A198, a German Fokker A two-seater of Feldflieger-Abteilung 40 or 41, at Rumbeke aerodrome, winter 1914-1915. The wings and horizontal stabiliser carry the Maltese Cross emblem (Collection Neil Reeb Belgium).

On 15 October pilot Leutnant Zeumer (who later became a close friend of Manfred von Richthofen) and observer Oberleutnant Schinzing explored the region around Roulers and Ypres:

The streets leaving Roulers and Iseghem in southern direction are free of enemy troops. A lot of rail traffic in the stations of Roulers and Iseghem. No enemy presence in Ypres.

Two days later, Hauptmann Hähnelt, commander of Feldflieger-Abteilung 4, made a complaint to the headquarters of the XIII Army Corps.

The squadron requests that it should be equipped with LVG-biplanes. All pilots can fly these aircraft. A note of 22 September 1914 mentions the arrival of the LVGs for the Feldflieger-Abteilung 4 in Trier. The unit also needs three additional LVGs. At this moment the unit has two Gotha-Taube aircraft, one Gotha biplane and one Albatros biplane. The latter is a training machine from the field at Montmédy. The squadron wants to hold its planes for action till the arrival of the new LVGs.

His letter sums up the problems the German air force faced at that time – not only were their aircraft obsolete but they were also in short supply – instead of six planes the squadron had been reduced to four as a result of two months' fierce fighting.

As aerial strength grew in the Fourth Army sector, crews of FFA 4 limited their reconnaissance flights to southern Flanders, as shown in this report of 23 October:

To the headquarters of XIII Army Corps
Crew: pilot Leutnant Zeumer and observer Oberleutnant Schinzing;
Itinerary: Lille (airfield) - Armentières - Ypres - Poperinghe - Steenvoorde - Hazebrouck - Aire - Merville - Estaires - Armentières - Lille

Time: 8.35 - 11.50 am
Observations:
1 In Ypres: two trains ready for departure heading south
2 In Ypres: large quantities of lorries and motorcars
3 A radio station to the south of Ypres
4 A lot of troops and convoys in the villages south of Ypres
5 No traffic on the roads from Ypres leading south and south-east

LVG BI of Feldflieger-Abteilung 1 outside a hangar in Menin, November 1914. Windows have been painted on the tent to make it look like a Flemish farmhouse (collection Decuyper, Belgium).

6 No enemy sighted in Poperinghe

7 Long convoys on the Steenvoorde – Hazebrouck road

8 A lot of munitions trains on the Hazebrouck – Bailleul road

9 A lot of traffic in Hazebrouck railway station: three trains departed, one after the other, in a south-easterly direction

10 An artillery unit heading for Morbecque on the Aire - Hazebrouck road. The head of the convoy near the letter U of Morbecque, the tail of the convoy near to the southern houses of Hazebrouck

11 We dropped bombs on the railway station of Hazebrouck

Location identification was done in a very primitive way – they looked on their map and noted which symbols, letters or numbers stood nearest to the objective. After landing they phoned these marks to the artillery – who would have had the same maps, and this gave them a reference on which to site their guns.

Point 3 was of particular importance to the Germans – it confirmed that the British already had wireless telegraphy and that their planes could send wireless messages to the station. At this time the RFC had one plane fitted with a wireless transmitter – an innovation the Germans would not introduce until mid-1915.

The report also demonstrates the new role in which the German air force was being used. Up to this point, patrols had a strategic purpose – to locate the enemy forces and report on their strength. From the 23 October, reconnaissance flights took on a more aggressive role: where is the enemy hidden? How can the air force help the artillery? How can the air force hurt the enemy? The number of artillery-spotting and bombing sorties increased to fulfil this role.

On 24 October Germany sent up a lot of aircraft – among them Leutnant Zeumer and Oberleutnant Schinzing, who went up to observe the heavy fighting around Ypres.

After dropping bombs on Armentières, they flew towards Ypres and were suddenly attacked by a French aircraft but without success, and the two Germans managed to get away.

The shortage of aircraft meant that the German command could never get a really clear picture of the disposition of the enemy forces and most of the time the artillery suffered from a lack of aerial support, as shown in a report of the 54th Würtembergische Reserve-Feldartillerie Regiment (Reserve Field Artillery) on 27 October:

We were in Ter Hand (near Becelaere) and fired on enemy batteries, which we could not observe because we had no aircraft.

However, aeroplanes were not the only way to provide range and direction for the artillery – there was wide use of observation balloons and even tall buildings or high ground – but these latter were not as versatile.

The capture of Ypres and the surrounding heights was an important objective for the German command, so a new corps was formed under the command of General

A German Drachen kite balloon. This Parseval-Siegsfeld balloon had a capacity of 800 cubic metres / 28,000 cubic feet, which was filled with hydrogen. Some eight such German observation balloons were active in Flanders during the First Battle of Ypres (Collection Raven).

Fabeck, tasked with effecting a breakthrough along the Menin-Ypres road. This corps consisted of XV Army Corps, II Bayerische Army Corps and the Bayerische Reserve Army Corps with two flying units – Bavarian FFA 2B and Prussian FFA 3. General Fabeck also could call on the flying groups attached to neighbouring armies: FFAs 6, 38, 40 and 41 of the Fourth Army, FFA 4 and other units supporting the Sixth Army.

The attack was planned for 30 October, and the day before Leutnant Schöller and Oberleutnant Sperrle of FFA 4 located enemy batteries, and also found troops on the Mesen-Armentières road and from the chapel just south of Zillebeke as far as the turn of the canal north-west of Voormezele. They found Ypres, Brielen and Vlamertinge crowded with troops and automobiles, and the roads were full of soldiers, so they dropped bombs on Ypres and returned home to report back to their own artillery. In accordance with the antiquated method of reporting back, when crew spotted enemy guns in the wood north-west of Zandvoorde, they reported the location as west of the number 40 on the map and 730 yards west of Hollebeke, near the number 58.

On the morning of the 30 October Zeumer and Schinzing were on a patrol. They landed around 11.30 pm and made their report:

1 A lot of infantry in Ypres

2 Concentrations of lorries and cars near Brielen, Boezinge and Elverdinge

3 A resting group of infantry near Brielen

4 Lorries transporting munitions on the road from Ypres to Sint-Juliaan

On 1 November, confident of success in the Battle for Ypres, the German Emperor visited Thielt and Courtrai to support his victorious army. More troops were massed for the attack and new FFAs were brought in: FFAs 5, 30, the Bavarian FFA 2 and 5 and last but not least FFA 1, which was assigned to the Imperial Guards.

Adverse weather prevented any reconnaissance flights during the massive German attacks on the Allied lines near Ypres on 10 and 11 November. Only from mid-November did weather improve, allowing flights to resume, and on 17 November the crew Vizefeldwebel Eberhardt

A French Voisin III. The steel frame construction of the aircraft enabled it to carry a bomb-load of approximately 330 lb/150 kg. On 1 November 1914, five French Voisins and one Morane Saulnier bombarded Thielt, where the German emperor was visiting – but without success. The aircraft carries the French flag on the horizontal stabiliser of the tail. Engine: 130 hp Salmson M9; wingspan: 14.74m/48 ft 4 in; length: 9.50 m/31 ft 2 in; loaded weight: 1,350kg/2,976 lb; maximum speed 105 km/h/65 mph (own collection).

and Oberleutnant Bernard of FFA 4 spotted an Allied battery on top of the Mount Kemmel, and Leutnants Rösch and Kraft of the Bavarian FFA2 B reported enemy infantry on the Bailleul-Ypres road, and identified a British airfield with twelve planes at Bailleul.

It was during the First Battle for Ypres that Germany started to improve communications between aircraft and the ground. At first observers had to wait until they landed to deliver their reports, but soon better and faster ways of communication were developed. Before the crew took off, the observer and artillery officers agreed what objectives they were to look for, and each was given a number. The crew would take off and fly forward beyond their own battery and then mark the target to be engaged by firing one, two or three flares. They would then turn just above the target, and this was the signal for the guns to start firing. When each round was fired the observer noted where it fell, then the plane came back towards the battery and gave the results by means of coloured flares – if the plane did not return this meant 'Fire again, we did not see the impact!'

Naturally both sides tried to stymie enemy reconnaissance flights, and on 1 and 3 November, Farmans of the RFC reported that they had chased away German reconnaissance aircraft. Another tactic was to shell the enemy's airfields to destroy aircraft or render the ground too pitted to allow take-off. On the 27 October German guns opened fire on a French observation balloon over St Jan near Ypres and on 3 November shelled the RFC's advanced landing ground at the same place. Four days later a raid by French Voisins on the German airfield of Rumbeke destroyed two planes of FFA6.

Despite improvements in air/ground communication, the German assault on Ypres failed. Wave after wave of German troops stormed the French and British trenches – but despite some small local German successes the Allies held their

ground, even withstanding an assault by the Imperial Guards. It became clear to Von Fabeck, commander of the group consisting of the XV Corps, II Bavarian Corps and three divisions, that he had got the support of sufficient numbers of FFAs too late to influence the battle.

The period between 11 October and 18 November saw a lot of aerial activity, with 172 sorties flown in support of the Fourth Army and 330 for the Sixth Army in France – and all this despite adverse weather conditions.

Sobered by his army's heavy losses and hampered by bad weather – there was snow from 12 November onwards – von Fabeck called off the attack on 21 November. Now his flying squadrons got new instructions – they were to penetrate enemy airspace and observe the enemy movements to try to anticipate their next moves.

There ensued a lull – an opportunity for the FFAs to improve their airfields and learn new tactics.

At that point the Fourth and Sixth Army in Belgium had airfields and first-line squadrons as follows:

Feldflieger-Abteilung	Commander Hauptmann	Flying for	Airfield
Sixth Army			
1	Von Oertzen	Winkler division	Menin (after a short stay in Gheluwe)
3	Genée	XV Army Corps	Menin
Fourth Army			
6	Dewall	AOK 4	Rumbeke from 23 October onwards
38	Volkmann	AOK 4	Ghistelles
40	von Körber	XXIII Reserve Corps	Handzame
41	Ruff	XXVI Reserve Corps	Staden (moved to Ghits on 20 November)

Units 4, 5, 24 and their Bavarian counterparts 2 and 5, supported the Sixth Army in France.

The First Battle of Ypres was over. Despite the use of more then ten FFAs – a quarter

*German Aviatiks of
Feldflieger-Abteilung 6
with distinctive Maltese
Cross insignia below
and above the wings in
front of the farmhouse
at Rumbeke airfield,
October-November 1914
(Collection Plane).*

of the total German aerial strength – the invaders had failed to break through and capture the strategically important region of the French Channel coast.

Pigeons as a Secret Weapon

Right from the British declaration of war in August 1914, the German High Command planned to carry out attacks against the English mainland. To this end, a man was appointed who would become one of the most famous chiefs of the German *Fliegertruppen* – Major Wilhelm Siegert. On the 19 October he joined the Army High Command as advisor on all matters relating to military aviation, and he immediately planned the formation of a bomber group at Calais which would be capable of bombing England. However, once Belgian troops had flooded the east bank of the River Yser in Northern Flanders, the German advance towards Calais was halted and Siegert had to rethink, and instead he chose Ostend for his new bomber unit. A suitable place for

their base was found at FFA 38's airfield at Ghistelles, and in mid-November work started to construct an airfield that remained one of their largest right to the end of the war. Overseeing the secret development were Oberleutnant Von Schröder and engineer Wegenast, and to preserve secrecy about the new unit, Siegert used a cover name: Brieftauben Abteilung Ostend (Ostend Carrier Pigeon Squadron) or BAO.

After the war Siegert described the construction of the secret airfield:

I always believed that we would capture Calais, which would enable our air force to carry out long-distance bombing raids. The new airfield had to be large enough to accommodate 36 aircraft and allow the simultaneous take-off and landing of a large group of planes. Our greatest problem was the fact that we had to drain the location. The nearness of the sea meant that the water level was just below the surface. A large part of the landing strip was metalled with

Hangars 13 and 14 at Ghistelles aerodrome, the home of the Brieftauben Abteilung Ostend. Four railway tracks enter the aerodrome, and rails connected all 20 wooden hangars. The area to the upper left is the entrance, with the lorry park and landing ground to the left (Collection UTD USA).

rubble and we began the construction of a wooden runway. These works lasted until the middle of 1915.

We built 20 wooden hangars, each big enough to take two or three aircraft, around the landing strip and painted them to look like the local houses to mislead enemy observers. Each hangar had electric light and telephone line and were all connected by rail to the local railway station, which enabled us to bring in the new planes by train.

On 27 November a group of 28 pilots and ten observers arrived for duty – the most experienced airmen in the German air force. Each pilot brought his preferred aircraft, which gave the unit a strange variety of pusher-planes, monoplanes and biplanes. The new unit would report directly to the Army High Command and was not part of the Fourth Army in Flanders.

The pilots and observers were accommodated in two large trains which, to avoid bombing, travelled every night to a small railway station some miles away.

But despite all the measures taken to avoid detection, Allied reconnaissance was bound to identify the new airfield eventually, and on 27 November a Belgian crew, Dhanis and Bronne, in a Henri Farman reported:

In the fields between Ghistelles and Snaaskerke we saw 18 aeroplane sheds and six planes...

The range of the aircraft available and the distance of Ghistelles from Britain still did not permit the unit to launch bombing raids against even the closest targets in England, so instead the crews carried out bombing attacks on important Allied targets in Belgium and France. By mid-December, through various reasons, Siegert could send only six aircraft to bomb Dunkirk, but gradually this number increased and by the end of the month, 12 aircraft attacked the French port. Siegert's dream of mass bombing raids against England had to be put on hold, and it would be 1917 before planes were produced with the range to bomb London.

The First Naval Air Squadrons in Flanders

On 23 August 1914, three weeks after the outbreak of the war and long before the German breakthrough in the direction of northern Belgium, the German Secretary of State, Grand-Admiral von Tirpitz, proposed the formation of the German *Marine Korps Flandern* (Flanders Naval Corps) from reserve German naval troops who thus far had contributed little to the war effort, tasked with occupying the Belgian coast. Despite strong opposition to from the German High Command, on 29 August 1914 it was agreed to set up an army naval squadron. This unit, under the command of Admiral Ludwig von Schröder, was almost 20,000 strong, but only the two naval infantry regiments were elite troops.

On the last day of August 1914 the first troops left Wilhelmshaven for Belgium, and in early September training started in Brussels. The German Naval Squadron's first action was against the Belgians on 9 September when, with III Reserve Corps and under command of General von Beseler, they attacked the important stronghold of Antwerp, entering the town on 11 October. Advancing steadily, the German Naval Squadron arrived in the coastal region of Belgium on 21 October, and Admiral von Schröder set up his headquarters at Bruges, in commandeered municipal buildings.

The Marine Korps Flandern finally came into being on 15 November 1914, when the Naval Squadron was amalgamated with a recently created second squadron under Vice-Admiral Schultz. The naval corps was responsible for the coastal area some 16 km/10 miles long between Dixmude and

The brand-new harbour of Zeebruges where a major German naval base was established in December 1914. In the background the long breakwater or 'mole' provided sheltered waters for the seaplanes to take off and land (own collection).

Nieuport, while the First Naval division under command of Vice-Admiral Jacobsen was to defend the Flemish coast between Nieuport and the border with neutral Holland.

In the Dixmude-Nieuport area the Naval Corps was protected against Allied attack by the flooded Yser River, and to the south the Fourth German Army occupied the rest of the front line. There was close co-operation between these neighbouring forces throughout the war, but Admiral von Schröder requested airborne support to strengthen the Naval Corps in the northern part of Flanders.

As the naval Zeppelins had not yet proved their usefulness, and as the German Navy didn't want to rely on land-based aircraft, they would have to rely on seaplanes for this support role, and the port of Zeebruges on the Belgian North Sea coast, with its almost 3.2-km/2-mile-long breakwater was the ideal location for seaplanes to operate.

Formed at Wilhelmshaven in northern Germany on 24 November, the *Marine*

Wasserflugzeug Abteilung (Naval Seaplane Squadron) headquarters moved to Zeebruges on 4 December, and a small squadron of three pilots, one warrant officer and 55 seamen, arrived three days later. Under the command of nobleman Oberleutnant zur See Friedrich von Arnould de la Perrière, the unit was tasked with patrolling the southern area of the North Sea and the coasts of Holland, Belgium, Britain and France, and to do this, they were equipped with two 120-horse-power Friedrichshafen FF 29s, numbers 203 and 204.

The small railway station on the Zeebruges Mole was quickly transformed into a hangar for the seaplanes, and two cranes that could lift two tons were installed, their arms lengthened so that aircraft could be lifted directly from the mole into the water. Out of the water the planes stood on specially constructed flat railway cars, and a locomotive was kept on standby to pull these off the mole so that the precious seaplanes could be hidden in the little village of Lissewege, 4.8 km/

3 miles inland, and two rapid steamboats were provided to recover broken-down or damaged seaplanes.

Almost immediately the small unit made front-page news throughout the German press when, on 24 December, one of the seaplanes piloted by Kapitän zur See Stefan von Prondzynski made one of the first raids on the British mainland, dropping two bombs on Dover, albeit causing little damage. Two days later he was awarded the Iron Cross Second Class.

Meanwhile, FFA 38 had left the north of Flanders, and because the Fourth Army was already short of air support the commander asked the Marine Corps for help.

A *Marinelandflieger-Abteilung* (land-based naval air squadron) was formed at Johannistal, in northern Germany out of personnel from the *Freiwilliger Marinefliegerkorps* (Volunteer Naval Flying Corps), and the new unit under the command of Oberleutnant zur See Egon von Skribenski arrived in Flanders on 21 December. At first the unit was based at Ghistelles, where they shared the airfield with the BAO, then the only bomber squadron of the German air force), then early in 1915 von Skribenski moved his unit of 113 men and six Albatros BIs to Mariakerke near Ostend, where he set up headquarters in the well-appointed Palace Hotel on the Ostend promenade.

Both units of the Naval Corps, the *Marine Landflieger-Abteilung* and the *Marine Wasserflugzeug Abteilung*, became part of the *Luftfahrtwesens des Marinekorps* (Naval Corps Air Service) under command of Kapitän zur See Hans Herr.

Zeebruges seaplane base. The seaplanes were kept on flat railway trucks which were pulled on to the mole by a locomotive to the cranes, which were used to lift and lower them to the water. The aircraft are two Friedrichshafen FF 29A seaplanes and one Albatros B, No 225. (collection Plane Belgium).

On 9 August 1915 the British lost the prototype of the DH2, shot down by a crew of II Marine Landflieger Abteilung near Beselare and brought back to the home base of Moorsele (Collection Raven).

1915

The First German Airfields in Flanders

During the First Battle of Ypres the Germans began constructing a series of airfields some 10-16 km/6 -10 miles behind the front line, and when winter was over, Allied reconnaissance crews found German airfields at Mariakerke near Ostend, Ghistelles, Handzame, Ghits, Rumbeke and Menin.

FFA 6, commanded by Hauptmann Dewall, reported to Fourth Army High Command, in which role it moved on the 25 October from Ghent to its new base at Rumbeke, a village near Roulers. The first Aviatiks arrived while farmers were still felling trees near the landing strip, next to which the medieval château of Rumbeke, headquarters of XXVI Reserve Corps. Hangars were built during December and January, and during the next two months the paintwork was undertaken – for which the local municipality paid the bill.

The finished aerodrome had six wooden hangars built around the farmhouse, concrete bunkers, workshops, a pigeon-loft, wine cellar, tennis court and baths.

During the fierce fighting in the First Battle of Ypres, FFA 41's first landing strip at Staden came under enemy fire, so Hauptmann Ruff moved his unit further away from the front line to a better location east of the village of Ghits, near the château and the Bruges-Roulers railway line, where three sheds were built for the six Fokker M8 monoplanes.

Observer Hermann Köhl remembered this period:

We were flying Fokker two-seaters powered by an 80-hp Gnôme, and we used them to drop grenades on the enemy. If we looked really hard, we could see the little clouds caused by the explosions, and in our imagination we saw the enemy running for cover. We were also issued with some 5- and 10-kg/10- and 20-lb carbonic bombs, which looked like huge drops. Our Fokkers could only carry two of these bombs at a time and it was a very risky enterprise, because with that weight aboard our planes climbed too slowly and could not reach a sufficient height. This only improved when we got biplanes, and then our 150-hp Albatros could easily carry 100 kg/220 lb to a height of 3,000 m/10,000 ft.

FFA 40, with its five Fokker M8s and one Albatros biplane, had its base at the village of Handzame, some 11 km/7 miles east of the front line at Dixmude. The airfield was situated east of the village on the grounds of the neighbouring village of Cortemarcq.

After the war, observer von Korb described one of the unit's hazardous flights:

Remains of a concrete bunker at Rumbeke airfield, photographed in 2001 (own collection).

Ghits airfield, the home of Feldflieger-Abteilung 41 – photographed after summer 1915. The double-track Bruges-Roulers railway line runs diagonally right to left, and on the eastern side of the railway are four large permanent hangars. The château was used to accommodate the pilots (own collection).

The landing T at St Denijs Westrem near Ghent, which was the base of Armee Flugpark 4 (Collection Nielebock Germany).

Two of our comrades are still in the air. The observer of the last plane that landed saw them shortly before landing, but now the fog is extremely dense. Everyone is worried about the missing crew. The whole unit has only one aim – to help that plane get home. At the end of the landing strip we set a haystack on fire, we fire flares which explode high in the air and we park the cars and lorries around the field with their headlights on.

At last we hear the engine of the incoming plane. We stare into the thick mist but can see nothing. Then the noise of the engine stops and the plane starts its glide towards the runway. Then suddenly we can see its dark silhouette. It is some 30 feet from the ground and is flying straight towards the high poplars. We all are in panic, but in the nick of time the plane raises its nose and the engine restarts. The silhouette disappears. We see the dark contours of the plane passing overhead brush past the huge cross at the cemetery... We light three magnesium torches. Again we hear the rumble of the approaching aircraft. We hear the engine stop. We see the dark shape of the plane, but he is to low. Two, three, four more times the plane tries to land – and then at last the big butterfly makes a perfect touchdown. The pilot, observer and the whole squadron are relieved.

During the war four airfields were constructed around the city of Menin, the first of which was established at the end of October 1914 for FFA 3 under Hauptman Genée in the neighbourhood called Coucou.

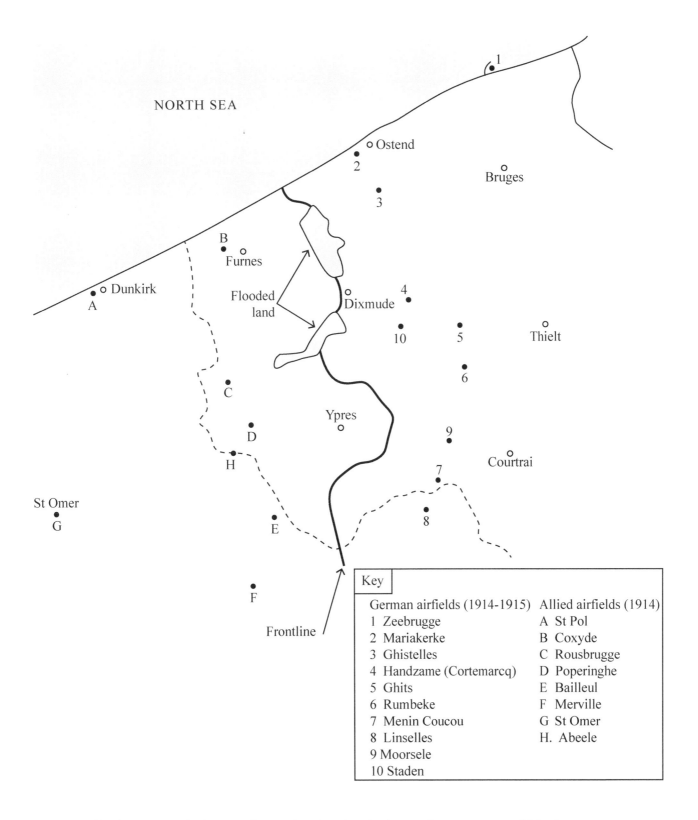

NORTH SEA

Dunkirk

○ Ostend
Bruges

Furnes

Flooded
land

Dixmude

Thielt

Ypres

Courtrai

St Omer

Frontline

1
2
3
4
10
5
6
9
7
8
A
B
C
D
H
E
F
G

Key	
German airfields (1914-1915)	Allied airfields (1914)
1 Zeebrugge	A St Pol
2 Mariakerke	B Coxyde
3 Ghistelles	C Rousbrugge
4 Handzame (Cortemarcq)	D Poperinghe
5 Ghits	E Bailleul
6 Rumbeke	F Merville
7 Menin Coucou	G St Omer
8 Linselles	H. Abeele
9 Moorsele	
10 Staden	

Occasionally the unit used also an advanced landing strip in the neighbouring village of Gheluwe.

In the first days of November the elite FFA 1 moved to an airfield just north of the river Lys in the south-eastern part of Menin, where they remained until January. They flew in support of the Imperial Guard Regiment which left Menin along with its airmen, after suffering a serious defeat by the British.

Flugplatz Handzame (summer 1916).
Six airplane sheds are built around the
farmhouse. Notice the shadow of the antenna
between the hangars and the landing T
pointing to the south-west(collection Plane
Belgium).

The other airfields were constructed at Ghistelles, Mariakerke and St Denijs Westrem. The Ghistelles airfield was some eight times the size of an ordinary FFA airfield. St. Denijs Westrem, west of Ghent, was the home of Armee Flugpark 4 (army depot 4), which was responsible for the supply and replacement of equipment and personnel to the flying units in the field, and was therefore sited some distance further from the front line than other airfields.

The Second Battle of Ypres

During winter 1915 the Western Front remained quiet as, for almost three months after the First Battle of Ypres, both sides directed their energy into consolidating their positions.

In the skies above Flanders the German air force had no shortage of enemies as it took on the three Allied air forces.

In March the Belgians divided their small air force into five *escadrilles* with airfields in Coxyde and Houtem near Furnes. At first they were equipped with Maurice Farmans and Henri Farmans, but by the end of February 1915 two Voisins bombers arrived, followed in May by the first fighter – a Nieuport X. At the start of May 1915 the British Royal Flying Corps had two wings active over Belgium, each with three squadrons. While the First Wing was not operational in the Flanders area, Abeele, a small Belgian village on the French border, was home to the Second Wing consisting of 5, 6, and 8 Squadrons, the Third Wing – 1 and 4 Squadrons – was in Bailleul and 7 Squadron was in St-Omer – both in France. Each squadron had twelve aircraft – but these were not always uniform – 4 Squadron flew seven BE2s, four Voisins and one Martinsyde. The French air force consisting of four escadrilles of six planes apiece, flew their Maurice and Henri Farmans, Voisins and Nieuports from airfields near Dunkirk, Poperinghe and Roesbrugge.

This brought the total number of Allied squadrons to 15, against some ten German units from the Fourth and Sixth Army – so the Allies were superior in numbers.

With regard to quality and performance, German and Allied planes were more or less equal. German aircraft had the propeller at the front of the engine, which meant that they were more agile and a little faster then the Allied planes. However, the observer sitting in the front cockpit had great difficulty using his rifle because the propeller, struts and bracing wires obstructed his field of fire. Allied planes were better adapted for aerial fighting because they were pusher biplanes with their propeller and engine at the back, which gave the observer a free field of fire in front of the plane. A significant difference however, was that even in the early days of the war, Allied planes were equipped with machine-guns, while German planes carried only a pistol or automatic rifle.

After the lull, the tempo of the fighting gradually increased again. In February 1915 the Germans launched an unsuccessful attack in the Soissons region of France, then the British launched an attack in Artois in France, having only a minor success at Neuve Chapelle. The Germans then planned a fresh assault to force a breakthrough in Flanders with the help of a new weapon – gas. Starting in March they installed gas cylinders in the trenches around the Ypres Salient and then waited for the ideal moment to storm the British and French positions.

What follows is a chronicle for the period between 1 April and 10 May.

Thursday, 1 April

The French pilot Roland Garros took of for a patrol from Saint-Pol near Dunkirk. He had become famous before the war having been the first man to fly the Mediterranean in 1913. Some time before he had set before his squadron his countryman Raymond Saulnier's plans for a system to fire forwards through the revolving propeller in front of

the plane. To solve the problem of getting the machine-gun bullets to pass between the blades of a rotating propeller, Saulnier fitted metal deflector blades to the propeller, so allowing the pilot to shoot through the propeller without damaging the wooden blades.

Above Furnes, Garros became aware of heavy anti-aircraft fire from the ground, targeted at a German Albatros. Garros gave chase and caught up with the Albatros about 10 km/6.2 miles from his lines at an altitude of 1,800 m/ 5,400 ft. He climbed in his Morane-Saulnier Parasol aircraft to a position of advantage above the enemy and opened fire with his 8-mm Hotchkiss machine gun at a range of 30 m/33 yd. The

German pilot headed for home and tried to escape the hail of deadly bullets while his observer replied with his rifle. The combat lasted some ten minutes, then finally, after Garros had used three magazines of 20 cartridges, the German plane caught fire. Spinning in the descent, the plane fell for about 20 seconds and crashed in flames.

On landing, Garros drove to the scene of the crash and found the plane and the burned bodies of the two German airmen in Oudekapelle. They were pilot Gefreiter August Spachholz and Leutnant Walter Grosskopf of FFA 40 from Handzame, where the airfield came under attack by Belgian aircraft which dropped five bombs from a height of 1,400 m/4,200 ft.

Saturday 3 April

To prevent further bombardments on the airfield at Handzame, the Germans positioned anti-aircraft guns to protect the landing ground and aircraft.

Easter Sunday 4 April

German aircraft continued to make regular patrols above the enemy lines. II MLFA flying from Moorsele carried out twenty sorties between 28 March and 3 April. However, due to adverse weather the unit could only do seven sorties the next week.

Tuesday 6 April

The Germans took all possible measures to prevent the Allies from detecting their build-up of troops with strategically placed anti-aircraft batteries. One of their victims was a Voisin of 4 Squadron RFC, that was hit by anti-aircraft fire above Houthulst Forest.

Thursday 8 April

Roland Garros forced down three German planes. A crew of I MLFA flew one of the planes that escaped the attack – Bootsmannsmaat Raschke and Fähnrich zur See Ratazzi managed to bring their crippled aircraft back to their home base in Mariakerke.

Sunday 11 April

Five German aircraft dropped bombs on Furnes, of which two were incendiaries.

Monday 12 April

German aircraft dropped seven bombs on Furnes. The British airfield at Poperinghe also got a visit during the night and bombs dropped by a German Zeppelin airship blasted craters in the Bailleul airfield.

Wednesday 14 April

Good flying weather. Between 11 and 17 April the German naval squadron based at Moorsele made 31 sorties, and this increased German aerial activity forced the British command to send three planes of 4 Squadron to Boulogne to protect the vital ammunition depot near St-Omer.

Tuesday 15 April

A crew of II MLFA from Moorsele made an unsuccessful sortie. Squadron leader Oberleutnant zur See Ritscher put in a report:

Early in the morning Bootsmannsmaat Reuber and his observer Fähnrich zur See Crüger, took off to photograph enemy batteries. They had just completed their task when a French plane suddenly attacked from behind the clouds. The enemy flew under the tail of the Albatros, and sitting in the front, observer Crüger could not swing his gun into a good firing position. The Frenchman opened fire and hit the Fähnrich zur See twice. Pilot Reuber received several bullet wounds to his chest, stomach, left hand and ankle. Well aware of the desperate situation, Reuber put his aircraft into a steep dive and landed in a field near Wervicq. The heavily bleeding pilot was brought to No 1 Field hospital of the Fifteenth Army Corps, but died three hours later. The next day, Fähnrich zur See Reuber was buried with full military honours in Moorsele churchyard.

The grave of pilot Ernst Reuber of II Marine Landflieger-Abteilung in the German Cemetery – the Soldatenfriedhof – at Menin to which his body was transferred from Moorsele, photographed in 2001 (own collection).

Friday 16 April

Belgian headquarters learnt from questioning German prisoners that a gas attack was imminent. This was relayed to the British and they sent planes of 6 Squadron RFC in search of any unusual activity. Captain Strange's aircraft took a hit in the fuel tank and he was forced to make an emergency landing.

Saturday, 17 April

Bad times for FFA 40 at Handzame. Pilot Wilhelm Wohlmacher and observer Joseph Seeboth encountered a British plane north of Boezinge – a BE2c of 4 Squadron RFC, piloted by Captain Vaughan with observer Second Lieutenant JF Lascelles. Combat started at a height of 1,500 m/4,500 ft, and the British pilot managed to get into a good firing position. Observer Lascelles fired 24 rounds at a range of 50 m/80 yd, hitting the German pilot in the heart.

The plane crashed near Phlypo's farm in Boezinge near Ypres. The 24-year-old observer Seeboth managed to take over the controls and landed in the French lines, where he was arrested by the French, caught in the act of burning important documents. A French report described the plane:

The aircraft is an Albatros biplane with a wooden fuselage around a metal frame. The power source is a six-cylinder water-cooled Mercedes engine. The aircraft carries two bombs on board. Most of the parts are of French origin.

As the German observer was taken away, another German plane bombed the château at Boezinge. The captured plane was later brought to Malo-les-Bains.

FFA 40 was not the only German unit to suffer losses that day. Further north another aerial combat went against the Germans. A Belgian crew, pilot Capitaine Jacquet and observer Lieutenant Vindevoghel, located German positions near Beerst, and in their slow Henri Farman they had great difficulty avoiding the anti-aircraft fire from the ground. Suddenly the shell-fire stopped and observer Vindevoghel, sitting in the front seat of the gondola, saw a plane decorated with big black crosses. The German pilot tried to get ahead of the Belgians to manoeuvre his observer into a good firing position, but the Belgian pilot quickly went into a dive allowing his observer to start firing. After only seven shots the German

A French soldier guards the body of pilot Wilhelm Wohlmacher by his Albatros at Boezinge on Saturday 17 April (own collection).

plane dived vertically straight into the ground, and this victory was recorded the first Belgian victory, the victims probably members of I MLFA.

German aircraft could no longer safely make patrols above the southern part of the front line, as every foray was met by fierce opposition from British aircraft. On the ground, the British were planning to capture Hill 60, a German position near Zillebeke which afforded good surveillance of the Ypres area. Deprived of aerial observation, the German troops were taken completely by surprise when the British attacked. The assault started as mines laid under the hill were detonated, then the British infantry stormed the position at 7.15 pm. The hill was in British hands by 2.30 am, although the two sides would continue to fight for this important summit for months.

Sunday 18 April
The German Zeppelins were making an increasing number of night reconnaissance sorties – so Lieutenant Hawker of 6 Squadron RFC took off and bombed the Zeppelin sheds at Gontrode near Ghent. Meanwhile, other crews of 6 Squadron on reconnaissance duty reported intense military activity at Wervicq railway station.

Also on this day, French aviator Roland Garros scored his third 'kill', and the champagne was waiting for him when he landed.

The British lost control of the heavily contested Hill 60, but eight RFC aircraft made an impact on events as, with the aid of their aerial reconnaissance and support, the ground troops regained it by the evening.

Monday 19 April
French air crews took off to disrupt the rail traffic behind German lines, and while attacking Lendelede railway station just north of Courtrai, one of the French planes had to made an emergency landing in the countryside near Ingelmunster, but is not

known if it was hit by German anti-aircraft fire or if its engine failed. On landing, the French pilot set fire to his Morane Saulnier Parasol L and hid in a ditch – where a German patrol found him. At first they thought they had captured a British officer, but his identity was confirmed after interrogation at the *Ortkommandantur* (local command post) at Hulste: the captured airman was the famous Roland Garros. The pioneering aviator and fighter ace was transferred to Menin where he was interrogated by the commander of FFA 3, Hauptmann Palmer.

This capture was a massive loss for the Allies – not only had they lost a legendary airman, but the Germans had gained important aviation technology – the armoured propeller. Suddenly it became clear to the Germans how Allied crews were able to fire forwards through their propellers, and they immediately commissioned their engineers to copy the system – and if possible improve on it. The arms race had begun.

Tuesday 20 April
German artillery began bombarding Ypres, and Allied reconnaissance crews went into action, quickly identifying massed German forces near the Houthulst Forest.

The Germans continued to shell Hill 60, and the position also came under aerial bombardment. Further west, German planes attacked the airfield at Bailleul.

Wednesday 21 April
Hill 60 again came under heavy shell-fire and the British infantry holding the position suffered heavy losses, however, the commander of 1 Squadron RFC sent up a radio-equipped spotter aircraft to locate the German artillery, and using information relayed back, the British artillery neutralised the German guns.

Meanwhile, 4 Squadron RFC moved to Bailleul in France, replacing 5 Squadron with the British III Army Corps.

Thursday 22 April

Throughout the day, Allied reconnaissance revealed significant German activity on the ground, then at about 5 pm Captain L A Strange of 6 Squadron RFC saw a plume of yellow-green cloud rise up over the line of the German trenches and drift towards the French lines. The deadly gas drove the French troops from their positions and the Germans stormed through the barbed wire to take the trenches, and crossing the Furnes-Ypres Canal, so that by 8 pm the German 211 and 212 reserve regiments were dug in on the west side of the canal.

The sky was full of aircraft, following the progress of the battle and relaying information to the infantry. Lieutenant Andrew of 4 Squadron RFC managed to take valuable photographs of the attack, and on the German side, FFAs 6, 40, and 41 and II MLFA accompanied the German attack. An observer from the latter, Fähnrich Sachsenberg took photos from a height of 600-800 m/1,800-2,400 ft, which gave vital positional information to the officers commanding the attack.

Friday 23 April

The gas attack achieved greater territorial gains than the Germans had expected, but short of reserves, they were not prepared to make a greater advance, and this prevented a major breakthrough. Despite the devastating effects of the gas attack, 6 Squadron RFC reported important news:

No important concentrations of enemy troops behind the lines.

For the time being they need not anticipate any attempt by German troops to make a major breakthrough.

Saturday 24 April

From their newly-taken positions, the German artillery was able to manoeuvre their guns to fire on Poperinghe.

Sunday 25 April

6 Squadron RFC was forced to leave their airfield at Poperinghe and withdrew to Abeele.

Monday 26 April

British aircrews discovered the armoured train which had shelled Poperinghe in the Langemark area. Guided by their reports, heavy artillery was ranged on it, quickly forcing it to move away.

During a reconnaissance flight, observer Köhl of FFA 41 had an extraordinary experience:

That morning the weather was very bad with low clouds, rain showers and a fierce wind – which was 'no-fly' weather. However, our headquarters requested urgent information on enemy movements, so despite the adverse weather Vizefeldwebel Lang and I had to make a reconnaissance sortie. Our commander Ruff had already left our squadron in the morning and was waiting for our reports in the Mannekensferme (Monks' farm) in the centre of Houthulst Forest. At 9.40 am we took off in our Albatros biplane. It was hard work – the dense layer of low cloud obscured our view of the landscape and when we dived through the clouds a surprise was waiting for us. Thousands of enemy reinforcements were marching towards the front.

We flew straight to our advanced headquarters at Mannekensferme and dropped a message, but due to the heavy rain no one saw it fall. Desperate, we returned to the front, where the situation had worsened. Enemy troops had already crossed the bridges over the Furnes-Ypres Canal. We had to warn headquarters. We landed near the farm where I requisitioned a horse to ride to the HQ. His Excellency General der Infanterie von Hügel and the commander of the artillery were there, and I gave a full report on the dangerous situation. Ten minutes later our artillery opened fire on the approaching enemy. The British counter-attack was doomed to fail.

Elsewhere German planes were driven away by Allied aircraft, and one German crew had to make a forced landing near Roulers to escape the enemy in the air. The RFC made several strategic bombing raids deep inside the enemy territory, targeting trains and stations to disrupt the German movement to Ypres. During the afternoon two planes of 7 Squadron and seven of 8 Squadron RFC took off from their field at St-Omer. Two planes were forced to turn back by engine trouble and another crew lost its way. Six aircraft bombed the stations of Thielt (four bombs), Staden (six bombs), Ingelmunster (12 bombs) and Roulers (two bombs).

A second group took off to bomb the railway stations of Roubaix and Tourcoing in France and Courtrai in Belgium. Only two planes of 2 Squadron reached their targets, and during his bombing run on Courtrai Station, Second Lieutenant W B Rhodes-Moorhouse was hit by German fire. Severely wounded, he managed to reach his aerodrome at Merville in France, but he died the next day. He was the first British airman to win the Victoria Cross for this act of bravery – only 19 members of the RFC and RNAS would receive this award during the course of the war.

Wednesday 28 April

II MLFA suffered its second loss. While patrolling above the Allied lines, pilot Bootsmannsmaat Möller and Fähnrich zur See Thalheim failed to see an approaching enemy plane as it closed in behind their Albatros S79 and opened fire. Observer Thalheim replied with his automatic rifle while Möller tried desperately to escape, but when Thalheim was killed and after the

engine was hit several times Möller had to make a forced landing just behind his own lines.

Thursday 29 April

I MLFA played an important role during the Second Battle of Ypres. The German command sited a massive gun in the north-east sector of the Ypres Salient, and crews of FFA 40 and I MLFA flew deep into Allied territory to direct fire. Between 26 April and 11 May 120 heavy 380-mm shells were fired on Cassel, Bergues and Dunkirk in France, and Poperinghe in Belgium.

Saturday 1 May

Good flying weather – the first in a long time.

Wednesday 5 May

After the successes of the German XXIII and XXVI Reserve Corps in the northern part of the Ypres Salient, the German XV Corps recaptured Hill 60 by means of a gas attack, forcing the Allies to retreat closer to Ypres.

Saturday 8 May

The Second Battle of Ypres was coming to an end, and aerial activity decreased above the salient. In the heat of the battle II MLFA flew up to 30 sorties a week from their base at Moorsele, but now this fell to around 24.

Sunday 9 May

FFA 3 was in mourning. During a patrol in support of XV Army Corps, one of their aircraft was shot down between Beselare and Voormezele. Hauptmann Hermann Thumm died near Hollebeke and his companion died later in Menin hospital. It was confirmed some days later that the aircraft had been brought down by an Allied plane.

Monday 10 May

The first German victory as observer Leutnant Wilhelm Frankl of FFA 40 shot down a Voisin with a carbine, for which he was awarded the Iron Cross First Class

1917. Later, because he was Jewish, the Nazi Party removed his name from the list of German aces.

By mid-May 1915 the Second Battle of Ypres was over. It had been a considerable disappointment to the German air force, having lost six planes and brought down just two Allied aircraft. Of the six planes lost, three belonged to the naval squadrons, and only FFAs 6 and 41 managed to escape loss during the battle.

Without doubt the exploits of Roland Garros and his secret weapon played a major role in these Allied successes, but the major reason for the German losses was that their aircraft were so underarmed. In these B-class machines the observer sat in the front cockpit under the upper wing and the wings, bracing wires, struts and high radiator obstructed his view and hindered him when he needed to use his carbine or pistol. German airmen had to rely on rifles, carbines and pistols, while the Allied aircraft were armed with machine-guns. Their only hope of a kill was if the observer was an outstanding sharpshooter.

Not only did the German observer have to defend his aircraft – he was responsible for photographing movements and dispositions on the ground. In his book *Du oder Ich* [You or I], the famous Theo Osterkamp described his first photographic assignments:

> *Two vertical rails were fitted to the side of the fuselage, in which a movable camera was fixed. This allowed the camera to be raised and lowered to change the photographic plates. High in the sky we had to do this after each photo we took, and that was no easy task. Even taking a photo was very difficult and dangerous. First, the observer had to kneel on his seat, looking to the rear. Then he had to put one leg outside the cockpit on the lower wing. In this position he would bend forwards to look through the lens. To take the photographic plate out of*

Photographed at Menin Town Cemetery in 1915, the graves of Hauptmann Hermann Thumm and Offizier Stellvertreter Karl Wippenfurth, of FFA 3, killed in aerial combat (own collection).

and later that year he was promoted to Vizefeldwebel.

Born on 20 December 1893 in Hamburg, Frankl was the son of a Jewish salesman. He became one of the first German air aces and on 12 July 1916 he was given the highest German award, the Pour le Mérite, informally known as the Blue Max. Later, as commander of *Jagdstaffel* 4 (fighter – literally 'hunter' – squadron) he notched up a total of 20 kills before he was shot down on 8 April

the camera and replace it with a new one, the observer needed both hands, therefore the pilot had to steer with only his left hand and to grasp the observer's belt with his right hand, so allowing the poor man to do his risky work…

All these difficulties made German planes very vulnerable, but already German engineers were working on solutions. The armed C-class and the improved version of Garros' aircraft were already on the stocks.

RFC Communiqués

On 25 July, Captain Hawker in a Bristol Scout attacked two hostile machines; one at Passchendaele at 6 pm and one over Houthulst Forest at 6.20 pm…

These were the first lines of the new Royal Flying Corps communiqués. From this point on, the British air force used this method to keep the home front informed, and these communiqués became an important record of the achievements of aerial operations during the war. Of course they were propaganda, and as such should be handled with caution, but they describe very well the introduction of new German aircraft.

25 July

Communiqué 1 continues:

…Both machines dived to escape. Captain Hawker then climbed to 11,000 feet and at 7 pm saw a hostile machine being fired at by anti-aircraft guns at about 10,000 feet over Hooge. Approaching down-sun, Captain Hawker opened fire at about 100 yards' range. The hostile machine burst into flames and turned upside down, the observer falling out. The machine and pilot crashed to earth southeast of Zillebeke in our lines.

From RFC Communiqué 2:

The machine brought down by Captain Hawker on the 25th was a large Albatros. It struck the ground upside down and burnt for a quarter of an hour. Only the wingtips, undercarriage, engine, and tailplane were recognisable. It could not be ascertained if a wireless had been fitted.

The frame of the tailplane, elevators, rudder, fin, and back half of the longerons were steel. Span of tailplane about 12 feet. Main spar and ribs of the wings were wooden with steel struts. Undercarriage usual 'V' type, with a heavy axle fitted with a brake in the middle.

The engine was badly damaged by contact with the ground, and by fire. The stroke seemed exceptionally long. The engine is thought to be a 150-horsepower Mercedes. It had two carburettors and two magnetos. A pair of Zeiss glasses, magnifying power 8, were found on the pilot, also a map showing the position of three hostile heavy batteries, and a copy of the Kölnische Zeitung of the 25th.

The grave and headstone erected to the memory of Hauptmann Hans Roser, in Sanctuary Wood Cemetery near Hill 62, Zillebeke (own collection).

The British were unable to determine from the wreckage if the aircraft was equipped with a wireless transmitter – vital knowledge because they already had introduced this innovation in their aircraft but were unsure if the Germans also had the technology. Already the British were finding wireless telegraphy very effective in carrying out artillery-spotting surveillance without wasting much ammunition.

Of course the Germans were aware of the advantages of wireless communication, and such was the demand for wireless-equipped planes that by the end of 1914 the *Inspektion der Fliegertruppen* (Air Force Inspectorate) developed a system to allow air-to-ground communication. The first viable apparatus was made by two firms, Hirth and Telefunken, and was successfully introduced in three FFAs in March 1915. Very soon all squadrons were equipped with two wireless sets – on 1 April II MLFA sent two aircraft to AFP 4 in Ghent to be fitted with the new equipment.

The set developed by Telefunken weighed some 15 kg/33 lb and had three wavelengths: 150, 200 and 250 metres. It had a range of some 40 km/25 miles and was therefore powered by a windmill-driven generator and a 37-m/40-yard bronze antenna which was suspended under the plane.

German wireless communication techniques improved during the Second Battle of Ypres. After the plane had taken off, the observer unrolled the antenna and gave a signal to the airfield. If everything was all right, the ground crew fired a Very light, then the plane headed for the front, where the observer tried to establish contact with their artillery's wireless station. Once they had good reception of the aircraft's Morse code signals, they laid out two large white cloths side by side on the ground. The observer would then give the number of the target and the number of the battery which should fire. The cloths were then laid out in the form of a cross shape and on seeing this, the observer ordered the battery to fire. The plane would then head toward the target and the observer would look for the impact of the shell and signal back the results.

Morse	Letter	Meaning
. - -	W	too far (*zu weit*)
- . -	K	too short (*zu kurz*)
- - . . - -	ZM	goal! (*Zielmitte!*)
. - .	R	the shell had fallen to the right of the target (*rechts*)
. - . .	L	the shell had fallen to the left of the target (*links*)

Each message was repeated three times, for example: - . - - . - - . - (R R R)

Messages might read as follows:

L 02 W 3: The shell fell 20 metres too far to the left and 300 metres too far.

This communication would continue until all targets were destroyed, and depending on available fuel, the aircraft could indentify a new target or return home.

19 September
Communiqué 11

Lieutenant Powell (pilot) and Air Mechanic First Class Shaw (observer), 5 Squadron, in a Vickers with a Lewis gun, when patrolling east of Polygon Wood at 6.00 am and at a height of

9,000 ft, saw a LVG at a height of 6,000 ft. The Vickers dived at the German, who also dived, firing upwards over its tail. The Vickers followed firing until he had dived so low that it was impossible to follow him further. He was last seen flying very low towards Menin. Immediately afterwards Lieuenant Powell looked round and saw a large machine (German) of unknown type coming up behind him. The machine was a three-seater with two engines, a single fuselage, and propellers behind the main plane with two machine-guns. The machine was very much larger than an FE2. Lieutenant Powell turned to engage it when it was about 100 yards away coming straight on and some 30 ft above the Vickers. The German was firing both machine-guns. When he was about 50 ft away, Air Mechanic First Class Shaw emptied a drum into him and he dived straight down, just over the tail of the Vickers. One of his engines had stopped and a cloud of smoke was seen coming from the other engine. Another machine was seen flying westward along the River Lys. When the Vickers turned towards him, this machine disappeared.

The large twin-engined pusher biplane the 5 Squadron crew encountered is likely to have been a Rumpler GII, powered by two 150-hp Benz or 100-hp Mercedes engines.

This type was mentioned in the diary of a sixteen-year-old schoolgirl from Menin.

Tuesday 7 September. This morning we saw an aerial combat above Menin: an English plane was attacked by five Germans but managed to flee.

A new aircraft arrived from Ghent. It has two propellers and two machine-guns. It is a real elephant….

Sunday 12 September. Late in the afternoon I went to the airfield. I saw the two big planes with their two propellers and their front and rear machine-guns. There is room for three airmen. We saw both planes take off but we did not see their return because in the evening, the guardsman had got new orders and forbade us to enter the airfield.

The girl was describing Menin airfield, where Feldflieger-Abteilung 3 was based. It was very unusual for an ordinary FFA to have large aircraft of this type, so the use of these planes by FFA 3 was most probably part of an experiment to use them in an offensive role. Seven days later a British aircrew encountered another large German plane – almost certainly an AEG GI or II, used as both a bomber and fighter. This plane had two propellers in front of the engines and was likely to belong to the BAO from Ghistelles or FFA 3 at Menin.

Lieutenant Sommervail (pilot) and Lieutenant Ryan (observer), 6 Squadron, when doing artillery registration near Zillebeke at 10.50 am, attacked a large double-tractor biplane which was travelling in a southerly direction at Hooge at a height of about 8,000 ft. When the machines met, the German was higher and opened fire from a machine-gun, of which he had two. Lieutenant Sommervail turned sharply to the left and then turned about to face the German. The machines then flew straight past each other firing with machine-guns forward, passing each other at about 68.5 m75 yd distance. The German seemed 200 ft higher. This was repeated three times. In all, 150 rounds of ammunition were fired at the German who had the advantage of being able to fire backwards from another machine-gun. The hostile machine then flew away in a south-westerly direction. On re-crossing the lines near Hill 60, a drum of ammunition was fired at an Albatros

An AEG GII of Kampfgeschwader I at Ghistelles. Introduced first in July 1915 and used in relatively small numbers, the GII was armed with two or three machine-guns. Engine: two 150-hp Benz Bz III; wingspan 16.2 m/53 ft; length 9.1 m/29 ft; weight empty: 1,450 kg/3,190 lb; weight loaded: 2,470 kg/5,434 lb; maximum speed: 140 km/h/87.5 mph. With a crew of three, its 200-kg/440-lb bomb-load was carried externally (Collection UTD USA).

over Sanctuary Wood. It turned away immediately and disappeared towards Gheluvelt. The German machine first engaged was a double-engine tractor biplane with large nacelle between the wings, mounted with machine-guns fore and aft, and with a lifting tail of the unstable type. The upper plane had laid-back extensions.

Captain Mansfield (pilot) and Captain Holt (observer), 7 Squadron, in a BE2c with Lewis gun, rifle and pistol, while on reconnaissance, engaged a German machine which was seen to come up from the aerodrome at Roulers. It was a double-fuselage machine with the observer in front and one machine-gun. After a brief exchange of shots at 137 m/150 yd, the hostile machine dived towards the ground apparently under control. The combat could not be continued as the sump of the BE2c was

shot through and it was only possible to cross the lines at 1,800 ft.

The last aircraft mentioned in the above report was less effective than the GII – the AGO C, which as a twin-boom pusher was something of a maverick among German aircraft. The two-seater biplane was very similar to the Farman designs – essentially the crew sat in a short nacelle with the engine and propeller at the back. Two booms supported the tail surfaces so that they cleared the propeller. A machine-gun mounted in the nose had a clear field of fire unhindered by the propeller, struts or bracing wires. The plane was used from the summer of 1915 onwards for reconnaissance duties, and although produced in limited quantities, the AGO C was often seen in Flanders during the winter of 1915-1916 where it was used by III MLFA, and maybe also FFAs 3 and 6.

26 October
Communiqué 16

Captain Loraine and Lieutenant Lubbock, 5 Squadron, in a Vickers Fighter on patrol near Houthem observed two German machines approaching from the east. The first was attacked and half a drum fired at him at a range of 15 yd. The German dived almost vertically, followed by the Vickers, whose pilot fired the remaining half-drum whilst the observer emptied nearly another drum at him. The German machine, an Albatros, was seen to crash to earth and turned completely over at square U13a56m, Sheet 28, within our lines. Captain Loraine then found himself at 700 ft and climbed to attack the second German. At 6,000 ft the engine of the Vickers stopped and Captain Loraine was forced to land. The pilot of the German machine was shot by machine-gun fire

and the observer was wounded and made prisoner.

Some days later the communiqués gave more information:

The plane brought down by Captain Loraine on the 26 October was an Albatros. The pilot, a corporal, was killed by rifle-fire. The observer, 2 Leutnant Buchholz was wounded in the head and is in hospital. He was only 17 years old and had won the Iron Cross when serving as an infantry officer in IX Corps. They belonged to the 33rd Flying Squadron attached to XXVII Reserve Corps. The 33rd Squadron is at Moorseele and consists of six Albatros machines, housed in wooden sheds. There are six pilots and six observers in the squadron. Casualties are replaced from Germany. Attempts to salvage the machine, which fell very near the trench line, were unsuccessful and during the attempt the Canadians lost two killed and two wounded.

The machine was fitted with a 6-cylinder Mercedes engine. The following have been rescued from it:

- a camera with trigger release for activating the shutter
- a pair of prismatic binoculars, 18-power, very clear definition
- a Mauser carbine, not automatic
- a Colt machine gun. This was recognised by the Canadians as one that they had lost last May
- about 100 rounds of Mark VII, 303, semi-automatic armament
- an ordinary aeroplane compass mounted in gimbals

The machine was not fitted with a revolving machine-gun mounting. A document found on the observer gave a summary of reconnaissance made during the past few weeks.

*An Albatros B after an
emergency landing near
Langemark, autumn
1915. The aircraft is fitted
with a captured Allied
machine-gun, operated by
the observer who sat in
the front seat behind the
windscreen (Collection
Raven).*

19 December
Communiqué 25

Second Lieutenant Finchan and Second Lieutenant Price (FE, 6 Squadron) attacked a Fokker over Bixschoote. The Lewis gun jammed with the first three bullets but then fired normally. The Fokker banked steeply and dived. In the meantime two more Fokkers were pouring rapid fire at short range into the FE from behind, and the petrol tank was pierced. Lieutenant Finchan banked the FE steeply to the left and engaged one of the hostile machines, which dived steeply. Its flight however could not be followed as two other machines opened fire from above. A drum was fired at the larger of the two machines but without apparent damage. The Lewis gun jammed again and the engagement was discontinued, the hostile machines following the FE no further than the lines. During the encounter, two Frenchman in a Maurice Farman endeavoured to assist the FE but unfortunately were brought down near Abeele, one of them being wounded.

Second Lieutenant Horsburgh and Lieutenant Haynes (BE2c, 7 Squadron) during a reconnaissance near Zarren were approached by three Fokker monoplanes which took up positions above, below and on the side of the BE2c. While these engaged the attention of the BE2c, a pusher biplane approached from the west and opened fire from behind at about 80 yd. Lieutenant Haynes replied with a drum from the Lewis gun. The petrol tank of the BE2c was pierced, necessitating the return to the aerodrome.

The report mentions two German planes: the new Fokker E monoplane and the AGO C pusher biplane. The Fokker E was equipped with an improved version of the Saulnier device that was fitted on

Garros' captured plane, and the deflector plates on the propellers were replaced by an interrupter mechanism which synchronised the machine-gun with the propellers. This meant that the fixed forward-firing machine-gun could fire between the airscrew blades. The Dutch aircraft designer Anthony Fokker had installed this system, together with a Parabellum LMG14 machine-gun on one of his Fokker M 5k (A III) monoplanes, which had previously been unarmed. On 23 May Fokker flew his single-seater to the front and demonstrated it to pilots and top brass, and Max Immelmann and Oswald Boelcke of FFA 62 at Douai were especially impressed by the demonstration. Initial orders were placed immediately and by mid-July, 11 armed Fokkers were flying in German units, and the Fourth Army received the aircraft in August 1915. However, the mechanism was not without its teething troubles, and on 19 September, Fokker E27/15 of III MLFA was non-operational due to malfunction of the interruption mechanism. The machine-gun had damaged the propeller during an operational flight by Flugobermaat Bödecker, who was the first naval pilot to attend the Sonthofen flying school near Mannheim, where he converted to the Fokker single-seater.

It wasn't until November that Fokker Es were delivered to most of the FFAs in Flanders, where it began to make an impact. Otto von Parschau of KG I shot down his first victim above Bruges on 19 December 1915.

The new Fokker would revolutionise air fighting but the Germans were slow to exploit the advantage the new plane gave them. The most successful version, the Fokker EIII, entered service in October 1915, but there were still only 40 of them operating on all fronts by the end of the year, and it wasn't until mid-1916 that all squadrons of the Fourth Army acquired one or more Fokker monoplanes.

The Heavy Bombardment of Dunkirk

During the winter of 1914-1915 the bombers of the BAO launched raids against the French ports of Dunkirk and Calais, with the objective of disrupting Allied supply routes, and if possible stopping traffic between France and Britain. However, Major Siegert, commander of the BAO, was hampered by a shortage of bombers, and it was April 1915 before he could muster 24 aircraft for a concentrated bombardment. Meanwhile Siegert reinforced his little group with aircraft from FFA 40 to carry out raids on 6 and 22 January. During these raids each pilot carried two bombs and the observers six, however, and most of the pilots flew solo so that they could increase their bomb-load.

The attacks were not without risks for the German crews, and on 22 January one aircraft failed to return from a raid, having had to make a forced landing. The pilot and observer were captured and made prisoners of war. A crew of FFA 40 experienced an engine failure shortly after take off and had to return home. Mechanics solved the problem and the crew took off again. The outward journey was uneventful – a report gives an account of the rest of the raid.

Dunkirk was in sight, and we flew above the railway towards the city. The observer hung out of the cockpit as far as he could and threw the first bomb. A cloud of dust and smoke showed us where it fell. After a second lap we were above the railway and station. The rails were undamaged. Now the plane had made a full circle and was some 100 m/ 300 ft lower. A second bomb fell... a third... a fourth... The railway track and a huge warehouse were hit. Our job was finished and we could return home. We stared into the distance and looked for an orientation point in the east. Flames blazed in the west and flashes of guns could be seen in the south. All of a sudden the engine stopped. We were still 15 km/10 miles inside enemy territory. Despite all our efforts we could not restart the engine. We glided in an easterly direction. We threw everything that was too heavy overboard. After a while we recognised the River Yser,

Fokkers E at Moorsele airfield. (7 April 1916, probably FFA 6. Left one wearing a big 2). The planes were powered by a single Oberursel U.0 7-cylinder air-cooled rotary engine (a clone of Gnome Lambda engine). Wingspan: 8.85 m/29ft 0in; height: 2.9 m/9 ft 5½ in; maximum speed: 130 km/h/81 mph; armament: one forward-firing 7.92 mm/0.312 in Spandau lMG 08 machine-gun (Collection Haerynck Belgium).

and we crossed the enemy lines at very low altitude. We flew through a hail of bullets but managed to land within our own lines. Immediately the plane became the target for all the Allied guns. We were lying in the mud, crawling from one bomb-crater to another until we reached the safety of our trenches. It took us several hours but the most important thing was that we were still alive.

Soon Siegert realised that it was too dangerous to attack Dunkirk by day – his slow and poorly armed planes were too vulnerable – so he adopted another tactic. From this point he would attack the French harbours only by night – and because he was well aware of the difficulties of nocturnal sorties, he himself took part in the first raid.

The attack on Dunkirk in the night of 28 January was an exceptional flight – it was the first night-time operation. The previous night adverse weather postponed the operation although one crew managed to bomb the objective.

At 11 pm, 15 planes took off, but one of these had to return due to engine trouble. The remaining aircraft bombed Dunkirk, but were hindered by the searchlights and shells of the anti-aircraft defences. We threw eight 10-kg/22-lb bombs and 114 5-kg/11-lb bombs. We all returned safely.

This attack set a precedent for Allied night raids against the Germans as a tough reprisal, and Belgian, French and British planes made regular raids on the German bomber unit's airfield.

On 1 April 1915 a Belgian crew found the airfield abandoned – Siegert had decided to move his bombers to other airfields on the front. The BAO transferred to new locations near Metz in France towards the end of February, returned for a short time to Ghistelles, then in March the squadron moved to the Russian front.

All transfers between airfields were made by train, which meant that the unit could move quickly from the one sector of the front to another. By mid-July trains had brought

LVG CII of Kampfgeschwader I. The number IV 1 indicates that the aircraft belonged to Kampfstaffel 4 (Collection UTD USA).

the BAO back to Ghistelles, but now the wagons carried new aircraft – 24 C- and G-types. The latter was the AEG GII – an armed twin-engined *Grosskampfflugzeug* (large fighter aircraft). The BAO also had a new commander – Hauptmann Gustav Kastner-Kirdorf replaced Siegert, who was promoted and moved to Headquarters in Berlin.

In August, the BAO was split, part of it going with Kastner-Kirdorf to the newly created *Brieftaubenabteilung Metz* (Metz Carrier Pigeon Unit), or BAM. At Ghistelles the BAO got a new commander: Hauptmann Freiherr von Gersdorff, and a lot of new airmen arrived from the Russian front. One of these greenhorns who entered service on 21 August would become Germany's most famous airman – Manfred Freiherr von Richthofen.

In Ghistelles von Richthofen met an old friend, Oberleutnant Georg Zeumer, with whom he had made his first flights. Zeumer's nickname was 'the Black Cat' because of his bravery and aggression, but now he was suffering from tuberculosis and had only one wish – to die in an aerial battle instead of dying in bed. Zeumer and Richthofen paired up as a new crew.

Although von Richthofen only spent a short time in Flanders, he always had good memories of this period of quiet flights, boring patrols and pleasant promenades on the beach of Ostend. He had only one disappointment – he didn't down a single enemy plane.

Von Richthofen left Ghistelles in mid-September, along with the greater part of the BAO personnel, who were sent to reinforce the support for the Third Army in the Champagne region.

Only a handful of BAO crews stayed in Flanders, fulfilling the same role as the FFAs – reconnaissance, artillery-spotting, and the protection of Zeppelins when they returned from their raids over Britain, for which latter they had a small number of Fokker

monoplanes. One of the pilots was awarded the Pour le Mérite after bringing down a British BE2c at Oostcamp near Bruges on 19 December – the first victory by a Fokker Eindecker in the Fourth Army area.

It was at this time that the BAO was renamed as *Kampfgeschwader der Obersten Heeresleitung Ein* (No 1 High Command Fighter Squadron) or KAGOHL 1, shortened to KG 1.

The Land-Based Naval Squadrons in 1915

In Mariakerke I MLFA was still busy improving its facilities when it was joined on 22 February 1915 by the newly-formed II MLFA. The two units worked together for about two weeks, then on 9 March Kapitän zur See Herr, commander of the Naval Corps, assigned II MLFA to operate under the command of XXVII Army Reserve Corps. A location was found near the village of Moorsele, some 24 km/15 miles from the front line, about 16 km/10 miles south of Roulers, and German pioneers got straight to work. Together with 50 civilians they prepared a 500-m/600-yd square runway

On 19 December 1915 Leutnant Parschau (extreme right), flying a Fokker E, brought down a British BE2c near Oostcamp (Collection UTD USA).

and built hangars for the first planes, which arrived at Moorsele on 20 March. Six days later the unit became operational under the command of Oberleutnant zur See Ritscher – just in time to take part in the Second Battle for Ypres.

The Marine Corps in Flanders now had two land-based flying units and in April 1915 the first squadron consisted of five officers, 18 NCOs and 83 men, and was equipped with six Albatros B1 biplanes, which they took into battle against some Belgian and French, but mainly British aircraft. The Albatros B1 was unarmed but in May the unit got six Albatros C1s. These biplanes were armed with a Parabellum machine-gun mounted on a pivot built on a rotating base, to be operated by the observer – however, this only provided defence to the rear, since the pilot did not have a forward-firing gun.

Another duty of the first squadron was to direct the Naval Corps' long-range guns, which were trained on Furnes and the other side of the front line. In his war diary, a schoolteacher from Furnes described these bombardments.

Monday 29 March. Two bombardments. No victims. At 8 am we can clearly see a German plane above the northern part of the town. It remains in the same place in the sky despite the heavy shooting of our anti-aircraft defences. Then at 8.30 am a coloured flare shoots from the plane and whirls downwards. This is a sign for the enemy, telling them that they could start their cruel work.

Some five minutes later we hear the cannon, followed by a loud screaming and finally our city is shaking with the explosion of the shell.

I MLFA's most important duties remained reconnaissance and bombing raids, as detailed in the unit's war diary for Tuesday 28 November 1916:

Very misty weather. In the morning four planes took off, in the afternoon only one. Two of these aircraft made patrols above the front, one carried out a long-distance reconnaissance flight and one made a bombing raid on Calais. On location L15 quadrant 20/25, they found 14 guns and one anti-aircraft position. Sluice three at Nieuport was opened to the sea between 10 and 11 am. The plane sent to bomb Calais encountered a Sopwith seaplane over the sea at La Panne and was later intercepted by two Nieuports and one BE-biplane. Our pilot had to fly to get away from them and landed safely at our base, but he still had all his bombs aboard. Later in the evening heavy rain prevented further flights.

Further south at Moorsele, the crews of II MLFA were operating above the Ypres Salient – one of the hottest spots of the entire war – and experienced tougher resistance. Flying in support of XXVII Reserve Corps, they had to patrol above the front between Beselare and Passchendaele, where they found it very hard to operate, and in early July 1915 their commander Ritscher sent a report to Naval Corps Headquarters in Bruges describing the deteriorating condition of his unit. The old unarmed B-category Albatros biplanes were much inferior to the new Allied planes, and he was promised better aircraft – armed C-category Albatros aircraft – and two AGOs, the S66 and the S158, were already on their way to Moorsele.

On 9 August II MLFA won one of its greatest victories. That morning a lot of Allied planes were in action, directing artillery fire on Hooge on the Ypres-Menin road. One of these was a brand-new British prototype – the DH2 single-seater pusher aeroplane, straight from the Geoffrey de Havilland factory – and pilot Leutnant zur See Maas and observer Oberleutnant zur See

Ritscher, in the unit's only Albatros C1, No 53, succeeded in shooting it down.

After the war Leutnant Theo Osterkamp (later a famous recipient of the Pour Le Mérite) recalled the events.

Finally towards the end of autumn our unit got planes armed with a machine-gun on a rotating ring, to be used by the observer. Now we had the weapon we needed to fight the enemy. Despite this, our infantry still complained that German aircraft fled from the enemy, and they were not wrong in saying this, since we could only shoot to the rear as the wings and bracing wires obstructed the observer's view to the front. When we attacked the enemy we had to dive at him and approach very close, then make a sharp turn away to allow the observer to fire at the enemy. Of course, this tactic appeared, as the infantry understood it, to be rapidly closing with the enemy with great élan, only to turn away and retreat at the last moment. Using this method only a lucky shot could bring down an enemy machine, and this happened to Oberleutnant zur See Ritscher and Leutnant zur See Maas

when they downed the aircraft of British pilot Captain Pike.

The plane was not hit, and the pilot had been hit just once in the head. He was buried with military honours and I myself undertook a flight to St-Omer in France to drop a message to the enemy in this respect. This was done, despite the fact that at that time this was forbidden by our headquarters.

The Naval Corps set up a new airfield near the coast on the road from Bruges to Wenduyne, between the two tiny villages of Neumunster and Houtave, where they constructed three wooden hangars. The airfield, known to the Germans as Flugplatz Neumunster and to the Allies as Houtave, would be the base for a third unit, III Marine Landflieger Abteilung.

The new base was ready on 20 July 1915 and soon the aircraft arrived that the unit had wanted for so long. As a *Kampfflugzeug-Abteilung* (Fighter Squadron) the unit was tasked with protecting the strategically vital coastal region between Bruges, Zeebruges and Ostend, where the deadly German submarines and torpedo boats were based.

Flugobermaat Bödecker in the first Fokker E1 (E27/15), Nuckhen (Caprice), of III Marine Landflieger Abteilung at Neumunster. The E1 had a rotary engine with seven cylinders (own collection).

With the German navy's repair docks, warehouses, bunkers and oil storage depots, it was a regular target for Allied bombers. The area was named 'the Hot Triangle', and submarines using the long canals between the ports of Zeebruges and Ostend to move to and from their shelters in Bruges, were particularly vulnerable to air attack.

The new aerodrome, Neumunster, was situated in the centre of this triangle, and from September 1915 the unit's four AGO pushers and one Fokker monoplane operated to give protective cover for I MLFA's slow reconnaissance planes and intercept enemy aircraft.

A typical operation took place on 19 September. Early in the morning pilot Obermatroos Arns and observer Obermatroos Dietzi started a patrol above the front line between Nieuport and Ypres. When they arrived in the area over Courtrai they were attacked by a Farman and a dogfight started which must be almost unique in the course of the war as it was a duel between two pusher-planes. Germany had very few pushers in service and used the pusher design with the propeller behind the engine almost exclusively for big multi-engined bombers.

After ten minutes of manoeuvring, the Farman closed in behind the AGO No S67, and managed to wound the German pilot who made a forced landing near Courtrai at 8.35 am. The Farman was also badly damaged, so he too had to make an emergency landing deep in Allied territory.

On that day AGO No S158 was also in action, escorting planes of I MLFA which were directing fire for the artillery, and the only Fokker of III MLFA got into a skirmish with a Belgian plane, during which the machine-gun got out of synchronisation with the propeller, damaging it. The crippled aircraft limped back to Neumunster where it was confirmed that the propeller blades had been hit by bullets in five places.

Throughout the summer of 1915 the seamen of II MLFA operated in support of the army. Requests by the Naval Headquarters to withdraw the squadron to

the north were denied until an army unit, FFA 33, arrived. This was planned for late September, and because the seamen had already left Moorsele aerodrome, the army had to rely on the neighbouring FFA 6. On 20 September II MLFA moved to Mariakerke on the Belgian coast, where it was absorbed into I MLFA under the command of Oberleutnant zur See Ritscher, and the reinforced unit then operated with 12 reconnaissance planes.

In Neumunster III MLFA was redesignated II MLFA (also known as a *Kampfflugzeugabteilung* – fighter plane squadron) and at the end of 1915 was reinforced by two agile Fokker aircraft. These were better adapted to the adverse atmospheric conditions caused by operating near the sea, and

Flugobermaat Bödecker summed up the problem with their aircraft in a report.

The AGO No LF67 needs nearly half an hour to take off from the sticky and muddy runway. Even with hard frozen ground this remains a problem for the heavy plane. The AGO is almost twice as heavy as the Fokker, and in addition its wings get destabilised by the wind and squalls. We prefer the Fokker, but there is an urgent need for a more powerful engine.

The following report demonstrated the importance of the land-based squadrons:

On 18 November 1915 a massive bombing raid was launched against Poperinghe in Belgium. All flying units of the German Fourth Army participated and five planes of I Marine Landflieger Abteilung took part in the action. During the attack a heavy snowstorm forced most of the 20 aircraft to return home and only three planes reached the target. Of these, two were from I Marine Landflieger Abteilung! They had managed to fly just out of the storm. The unit received congratulations from German Fourth Army Headquarters.

German Seaplanes in 1915

At noon on 17 December 1915 a German seaplane made an emergency landing off the coast of Nieuport, where both crew members were captured by a French ship and brought to the port of Dunkirk, where they were interrogated. Notes from this interrogation provide an insight into the organisation of the German naval base at Zeebruges.

Headquarters, 19 December 1915.
Interrogation of the prisoners
Fritz von Arnould, Oberleutnant zur See, 27 years old, pilot. Hans Virchow,

Leutnant zur See, 23 years old, observer. Both men claimed to be newcomers to the seaplane squadron at Zeebruges.

Circumstances of their capture
They had left Zeebruges on 17 December at 1.45 pm together with two other seaplanes. Due to engine trouble they were forced to land on the sea off the Belgian port of Nieuport, where a French torpedo-boat had captured them.

The naval base at Zeebruges
Created by the headquarters of the Naval Corps, it is a part of II Marine Flieger Abteilung active in the North Sea. Other bases of this Abteilung are in Heligoland and Borkum (both in Germany). The first operates in

the Baltic Sea – other naval facilities are at Wilhelmshaven und Kiel. The distribution centre is at Warnemünde. Zeebruges has only four seaplanes, one of which is not operational. The seaplane shot down on 14 December was one of these four aircraft.

Duties
There are no specific duties for the seaplane station at Zeebruges. Most of their operations are reconnaissance flights over the sea. The pilot had already made three such flights, the observer one. The flight of 17 December was to trace enemy monitor warships.

The planes above Zeebruges may also make bombing raids. The observer had made a training flight during which, from a height of 400 to 500 feet, bombs were thrown at a target 5 x 10 yd. However, there have been no bombardments on Belgian or French soil.

In the captured plane notes on the positions of our vessels were found. This proves the close co-operation between submarines and seaplanes.

Captured Aircraft
Our troops are still trying to recover the enemy seaplane. Manufacturer: Friedrichshafen-Wasserflugzeug Baugesellschaft (Friedrichshafen Seaplane Construction Company) at Johannistal (Germany). It is a two-seater twin-float reconnaissance biplane with a 150-hp six-cylinder water-cooled Benz

The shelling of the seaplane base at Zeebruges, August 1915 (Collection Raven).

engine. Propeller: Reschke. Petrol-tank: 250 litres. Speed: 100-150 km/h. All seaplanes in Zeebruges are of this type, except one Albatros.

The plane is equipped with a transmitter and a machine-gun. All planes in Zeebruges are armed with a machine-gun. Pigeons are used as messengers – a wicker basket containing two pigeons was found in the captured aircraft.

Signals
The seaplanes carry white, red and green flares. The white ones are used for emergency landings, green ones signify that everything is OK, red ones for danger.

Balloons
Weather balloons (60 cm diameter) are released to measure the wind and to determine its direction. The prisoners do not know if big balloons are used for shooting practice.

Miscellaneous
Zeebruges
Our bombardment of the Zeebruges Mole didn't cause much damage. The aircraft shelter on the mole is bombproof with steel and concrete parts. The observer confirms that there are no anti-aircraft guns on the mole, which is borne out by the results of our reconnaissance of 8 November 1915.

Heligoland
The seaplane base of Heligoland has seven or eight aircraft.

Railways
One of the prisoners described his journey from Berlin to Zeebruges. He left Berlin on 9 December at 8 pm and travelled via Cologne and Brussels, arriving in Bruges the next day at 4 pm.

The other said that he too came from Berlin. He remembers departing in the morning and arriving during the night. Signed, Chief of Headquarters, Desticker

The two German prisoners tried to fool their Allied interrogators with misinformation, understating the number of planes at Zeebruges and Heligoland and claiming that they were two greenhorns, but von Arnould was one of the founders of the Naval Seaplane base at Zeebruges. The Allies were unaware of his importance – von Arnould was commander of the base and not an inexperienced flyer – which makes it hard to understand why he was so easily captured by the French, especially when it emerged that another German seaplane had landed by the side of his aircraft, giving von Arnould the opportunity to escape.

The capture of their commander was a major setback for the Zeebruges base. Under von Arnould's command the seaplane base had become a dangerous wasps' nest for the Allies in the North Sea and the Channel. It was the jewel in the Flanders Marine Corps' crown – and therefore the focus of many visits by German dignitaries, including the King of Saxony, who inspected the base on 25 March 1915.

Work went on all the time to improve the Zeebruges seaplane base. At first the seaplanes stood in the open air so they were subject to the bad weather and the salt air on the mole. During 1915 there was constant building activity – hangars for the planes, workshops, quarters for the men, a kitchen and a canteen.

Not only was the Zeebruges Mole important for the seaplane base – there was also the railway line to Bruges, by which the seaplanes were moved in and out, as every night a train loaded with seaplanes carried them to cover in the nearby village of Lissewege, where the school next to the station was commandeered and became a central workshop run by *Chef-Ingenieur der Reserve* (Reserve Chief Engineer) Doktor Ingenieur Stein.

As well as bombing Allied shipping and raids on the British coast, the German seaplanes monitored maritime traffic to Holland, which stayed neutral during the war and, because of its position between belligerent countries, could only could bring imports in by sea. They were also tasked with protecting their own submarines and ships, and last but not least, they carried out reconnaissance sorties.

On 11 March 1915 the unit's war diary recorded:

Training and reconnaissance by seaplanes 204, 208, 285 and 406. Report: the coast between Calais and Hoek van Holland and Schauwenbank is free of enemy ships. An English ship was bombed. One of the planes flew escort to protect our minesweepers.

Throughout 1915 the German seaplanes always flew away, avoiding any combat with Allied aircraft, which meant that there were very few encounters recorded. The slow seaplanes, armed only with the observers' machine-guns, always flew very low above the waves, preventing any attack from below.

With von Arnould a prisoner of war, Kapitänleutnant Walther Faber assumed command for a short time, but was killed in aerial combat on 6 January 1916, after which Kapitänleutnant Bernhard von Tschirschky und Bogendorf took command of the base.

A captured Allied Nieuport, repainted in the colours of II Marine Landflieger Abteilung at Neumunster. The unit used this plane on numerous occasions as a decoy against Allied aircraft, and on 5 May 1916 it was in action alongside Fokker Eindeckers that they brought down a French Caudron. From September 1915, Belgian crews filed reports of dogfights against a Nieuport in German colours (own collection).

1916

The German air force in Flanders began 1916 with eight units – the two naval squadrons in the coastal area at Mariakerke and Neumunster, and the remainder of the KG 1, the former BAO, at Ghistelles. In the centre of the province, FFA 40 operated from the airfield at Handzame, FFA 41 from Ghits and FFA 6 from Rumbeke. In the south FFA 33 remained at Moorsele and FFA 3 at Menin.

All this changed in 1916, as new units arrived and new airfields were built to accommodate them. In summer, as the battle intensified in France, the German High Command deployed most of the FFAs to the areas of heaviest fighting.

At the start of the year German planes had the edge over their Allied counterparts – the Fokker monoplanes were still effective – however, this changed during summer 1916, and the German command needed to equip the pilots with more agile aircraft and create specialised fighter squadrons to regain the upper hand.

Flying for the Artillery

At the start of 1916 the German air force consisted of more then 80 FFAs, but this was still not enough to handle the increasing burden of duties they had to fulfil. Originally operating as observation and reconnaissance units, they now took on photographic work, bombing, aerial fighting and artillery-spotting, and as specific aircraft were developed for these different duties, the German High Command ordered the formation of specialised flying units.

In October 1915 the first *Artillerie Flieger Abteilungen* (AFA – squadrons flying for the Artillery) were formed. These squadrons were some hundred men strong and equipped with four aircraft fitted with wireless transmitters, to send Morse signals to two stations on the ground.

A note from the German headquarters set out the duties of the AFAs:

The AFA provide a vital service for the artillery, and all artillery commanders must co-operate and avail themselves of the advantages the Artillery Flieger-Abteilungen can give them. The best way to do this is for the AFA to fly missions above the front line and direct artillery fire from the air.

For their part, the Artillery Flieger-Abteilungen need to have a comprehensive knowledge of how the artillery works, and the different types of artillery fire and when best to use them, and of the different types of shells and calibres. It is also imperative that they are fully competent in wireless communication, observation and photography.

Both artillery and the AFA must trust each other and co-operate fully to get the best results.

The number of these AFAs increased from 15 at the end of 1915 to 50 a year later, and by the end of 1917 this had grown to 105.

In December 1915 AFA 209 was the first to arrive in Flanders, brought in by rail to its newly-built airfield at Beveren, just north of Roulers. In January AFA 213 joined FFA 3 at

(Above) Personnel of AFA 213 in front of a railway car transporting mobile wireless stations with their antenna (Collection Tholl USA).

(Right) Ground wireless operators of AFA 213 using a portable set, early 1916 (Collection Tholl USA).

(Below) AFA 213 at Menin-Coucou, early in 1916. When weather was fine wireless operators worked in open air (Collection Tholl USA).

Menin-Coucou and the Bavarian AFA 102B took over a base on the other side of Menin. All three units were greenhorns and gained their first experience of the front in Flanders.

In early February AFA 209 left Beveren at short notice to take part in the German assault at Verdun, and it was not until the end of April that AFA 226 came from the Russian front to replace it.

Two new airfields were built for the AFAs and these, like all the other aerodromes, were built on requisitioned farmland. The first was south-west of Beveren, a little village that housed the headquarters of XXVI Reserve Corps. All the airfield buildings and tents were clustered around the farmhouse, which stood on the road to Roulers.

The second airfield was set up on the outskirts of Menin in the neighbourhood known as 'the barracks'. The rectangular airfield ran east-west between the River Lys and the French border, with the tents, main station building and work-sheds on the east side near the farmhouse. From 24 June the airfield was home to FFA 57, which transferred from Poland. The Germans called the airfield Flugplatz Halluin after the nearby French village, but it was later renamed as Menin Ost.

Since mobilisation the FAs were allocated to the armies and army corps, and now the German High Command tried to assign an AFA to every division – although this couldn't be achieved until the middle of 1917. At this stage only a few divisions got their own AFA, and at the end of 1916 XIII Army Corps had FFA 3, but only one of its two divisions, the 27th, got the support of an AFA, number 213.

Although the AFAs were the main source of range-finding for the artillery, they were soon given additional roles – carrying out bombing raids against strategic targets behind the front line, and a new fighter role for which they were equipped with Fokker monoplanes.

AFA 213 was formed in late December 1915 and arrived in Menin, its first operational aerodrome, in January 1916. It comprised four pilots, four observers, five mechanics, five wireless operators and some 80 other support personnel, and was equipped with four LVG CIIs. The unit, under the command of Hauptmann Böhmer, covered a huge area of the Ypres Salient in support of the German 27th Division. Quickly into action, on 10 February 1916 one of the unit's aircraft flew the first patrols against Allied planes, and it was on 9 March that AFA 213 celebrated its first victory when Unteroffizier Gröscher and Leutnant Patheiger downed a British Morane Parasol north of Wijtschate. The second success followed on 1 April, when they shot down a British BE2.

Observation balloons were always prime targets and on 9 July a huge operation was launched against four Allied balloons, three of which were situated north of Poperinghe, the fourth west of Mount Kemmel. The operation involved several units, each with a specific objective. Three Fokker monoplanes of FFA 6 were detailed to destroy the balloons by diving on them from a high altitude. Three LVGs of FFA 3 were to draw the Allied anti-aircraft fire, and two LVGs

of AFA 213 were to take out the Allied anti-aircraft guns.

The whole operation failed due to quick reactions by the Allies, who managed to ground the balloons in time to avoid attack, and furthermore no anti-aircraft batteries were destroyed because they didn't reveal their positions by opening fire.

AFA 213 was kept very busy throughout the year, and although they flew a wide variety of missions, their main objective was to locate enemy batteries, as in the following reports:

6 September 1916. Vizefeldwebel Rode and Leutnant der Reserve Grossmann took off at 1.15 pm on a photographic sortie. They took 16 photos of British positions to the south of Ploegsteert Forest. They were attacked above Wulvergem by an Allied Rumpf biplane [an aircraft with linen-covered fuselage], but they were back home by 3.08 pm.

24 September 1916. Late in the morning the same crew took 28 photos of

An LVG CII at Moorsele aerodrome, January 10, 1916 – one of the most successful two-seaters used by the Germans during 1916. It had a 160-hp Mercedes DIII engine – only the crankcase being covered by curved metal decking. The windmill-driven generator under the fuselage provides power for the wireless. The LVG was armed with a Parabellum machine-gun manned by the observer, and some models had a forward-firing Spandau machine-gun. The pilot sat on the main fuel tank, which was shaped to provide a seat. The LVG CII was capable of speeds up to 130 km/81 mph and had an endurance of four hours (Collection Haerynck Belgium).

*British batteries from an altitude of 4,200
m/13,800 ft. They were hampered by
heavy anti-aircraft fire and pursued by a
Gitterschwänze [an aircraft with a fuselage
made of steel tubing] and they fled after
they got a bullet in the petrol tank.*

Both sides made increasing use of
wireless telegraphy to make reports from
above the front, and valuable information
was to be gained by intercepting these
reports. Both Germany and the Allies
set up listening stations. The Germans
called them *Funkenstationen* (wireless
stations), and every one had one or more
Fliegerwarnungsstationen (aeroplane warning
stations), whose task it was to intercept the
enemy's Morse signals and, if possible, learn
the intentions of the Allied artillery.

During 1916, Funkenstation 5 was active
in southern Flanders. It was consisted of two
aircraft warning stations – one in Beitem just
south of Roulers and one in Gheluwe along
the Menin-Ypres road.

The Battles of Verdun and the Somme

In December 1915 the German High
Command launched an offensive to take
the French stronghold at Verdun in the
Ardennes. Well protected by modern
defences, this town was a crucial cornerstone
of the French front line between Luxembourg
and the Swiss border.

In the months leading up to the battle,
which began on 21 February, the German
Army amassed a large concentration of guns,
troops and supplies and had brought most of
the air force into the region.

There was only one FFA from the Fourth
Army sent to the Verdun region. In early
January 1916 AFA 209 left Beveren to give
support to the Fifth Army near Verdun,
where its four aircraft worked with the heavy
artillery to enable the German capture of the
important French stronghold of Douaumont.

The second unit to leave Flanders was
the bomber group KG I, which moved from
Ghistelles to Rethel in France between 5 and
11 February, its 36 aircraft flying to their
new location and the personnel moving in
by train. KG I and KG II were engaged in
bombing raids against railway junctions
and aerodromes behind the French lines,
and were so successful that the German
High Command decided to create four new
KGs: III, IV, V and VI, all with 36 planes
except KG VI which had only half that
strength. This force of some 200 bombers
caused enormous damage and seriously
hindered the transport of French supplies and
reinforcements.

Despite the heavy German presence in the
air, the French regained aerial superiority,
and such was their impact that the German
command now decided to use their large
force of KG planes in a fighter capacity
against the French raiders – but in doing so
made two mistakes. Firstly this detracted
from their massive bombing operations,
so allowing the French to build up strong
reserves, and secondly the large two-engined
G-type aircraft were not suited to their new
fighter role and were outclassed by the faster
and more agile French Nieuport fighters –
and consequently suffered significant losses.

During the Battle of Verdun the flying
units of the German Fourth Army launched
a series of bombing raids against strategic
Allied targets, designed to fool the Allies into
thinking that KG 1 was still in Flanders.

On 13 February planes of all the
squadrons attached to the Fourth Army,
including two aircraft of AFA 213 and five
from the Marine Feldflieger-Abteilung,
attacked Poperinghe. A week later the
Bavarian AFA 102B took part in another
raid – which ended in disaster for one of
its crews. The pilot, Vizefeldwebel Weber,
described the mission:

*In the moonlight all our unit's aircraft
were ready to start. Together with other*

Feldflieger-Abteilungen they were to take part in a large bombing raid on Poperinghe. At 6.45 am a Very light lit up the sky above the horizon and some minutes later a second rocket gave the signal to start. The first machine took off, followed by another and another at half-minute intervals. We followed the leader.

Flying in circles above Menin and Wervicq we climbed to 2,500 m/ 8,000 ft, at which I detected an engine malfunction. It would have been impossible to follow the other aircraft to a higher and safer altitude, and we were having great difficulty following the faster planes, so I decided to fly straight to Poperinghe. We crossed the lines unseen by the Allied anti-aircraft defences and soon reached our target. My observer Zeileis dropped our bombs and we started our second duty, which was to search for the location of the enemy's heavy artillery.

All of a sudden Zeileis knocked on my helmet. At the same time I heard the rattle of a machine-gun. Almost simultaneously I threw my aircraft

into a right turn. To the left above us and somewhat higher, I saw a Morane-Saulnier. Zeileis fired continuously at our attacker. Right in front of us I spotted British biplanes heading towards us. I forced the nose down to get greater speed but then encountered three more enemy aircraft. We had to fight.

I made another turn to the left and noticed that my observer had stopped firing. In my rear-view mirror I could see his body sunk down in the cockpit, his right hand lying on my shoulder. I had to take to my heels. I made a steep dive for some 700 m/2,000 ft and started gliding towards our lines at a height of 2,500 m/8,000 ft. The Morane-Saulnier was still following us and his bullets hit my plane several times. I was still 13 km/8 miles inside Allied airspace when all of a sudden I felt a hard kick on my right shoulder. Blood was running out of my sleeve and I had lost all feeling and power in my right arm. I had to reach home at any cost.

Then my propeller stopped... my fuel tank was empty. With a great effort I took the control between my knees *and pumped the reserve fuel with my good arm. At last the propeller restarted and finally we reached our own lines, where our pursuer had to turn back. I continued in a straight line, gliding down to our airfield, and landed smoothly… I was saved… but for my observer all help came too late.*

On 22 February FFA 33 bombarded the French port of Dunkirk. After the war Hermann Köhl, commander of FFA 41, explained the purpose of these flights:

One particular tactic we adopted was mass bombing raids against important Allied targets. We brought together aircraft from all squadrons to form large groups – these bombardments had to distract the attention of the Allies so they did not became aware of our preparations for the assault on Verdun.

Starting simultaneously, assembling in the air and flying in close formation gave us a lot of problems, and the bombing itself was somewhat chaotic as we frequently released our bombs either too early or too late.

The Allies responded to our raids by increasing the number of anti-aircraft guns so we had to fight our way back amid hundreds of exploding shells.

The biggest joint British and French offensive of the war – the Battle of the Somme – began early on 1 July 1916. Two British armies and one French would launch an attack to relieve the pressure on the French Army at Verdun. Allied aerial strength was almost three times that of the German Second Army, and they were equipped with high-performance fighter aircraft, capable of seeing off any German opposition.

This situation demanded an immediate strengthening of the German air force and AFA 102B and FFA 57 were sent from the Fourth Army as reinforcements. Aircraft of the first unit flew directly from Menin to Ham in France, while the planes of FFA 57 were brought in by lorry to their new location on 13 July.

Meanwhile the crews of the Fourth Army scored their greatest success of the war. Reconnaissance flights had revealed a major ammunition dump in a little French village near St-Omer. This target was more then 60 km/40 miles inside Allied territory on the railway line from Calais to St-Omer, and FFA 40 was sent on a night mission to destroy it. Four aircraft left the aerodrome at Handzame with a combined bomb-load of about 770 kg/1,650 lb bombs.

During the night of 20/21 July we made a bombing raid. The flight itself posed a great challenge to us because we had to penetrate deep inside the Allied lines and we had great difficulty finding our way above enemy territory in the dark.

Our little formation attracted many searchlights but finally we found our objective. It was a large British munitions factory, surrounded by a lot of large ammunition sheds. When we arrived at 3 am the whole factory was illuminated but when I, in the last plane, flew over the target it had disappeared into the darkness. Now the only light came from searchlight beams and the exploding anti-aircraft shells.

We circled above the factory for seven minutes, throwing our bombs, blinded by the searchlights and not knowing if we were hitting the target. It wasn't until we'd turned for home that we saw the beginnings of a fire at the factory. Almost immediately the little fire turned into a tornado of explosions and flashes. We still could see it blazing as we were gliding down to our airfield some 80 km/50 miles away from the destroyed factory. Now and then munitions exploded, sending fireballs high into

The large British ammunition dump at Audruicq, between St-Omer and Calais. On the night of 20/21 July 1916, four aircraft of FFA 40 destroyed the dump – photos were taken by a crew of FFA 6 (own collection). Picture below: After the bombardment.

the sky. As soon as I landed, I learned that it was my observer who had set the factory on fire. Several days after the raid we could still see a large mushroom of smoke above the bombed site.

The loss of such a large quantity of ammunition and the factory was a severe blow to the British.

On 29 August Field Marshal von Hindenburg succeeded General von Falkenhayn as Commander of the German armies. Assessing the situation, von

Hindenburg realised that his forces were over-extended, and to resolve this problem he decided to stop the offensive at Verdun and instead to reinforce his army at the Somme. The Fourth Army now had to send most of its flying units to the danger zone.

By this time FFA 41 had moved to Flesquières in the Second Army sector. On

German mobile anti-aircraft guns near the coast (own collection).

6 September FFA 3 moved to the Somme and the next day AFA 226 transferred from Beveren to Noreuil. Also in September, FFAs 6 and 40 left the Fourth Army, shortly followed by AFA 213 on 1 October.

These movements significantly weakened the aerial strength of the Fourth Army as only FFA 33 in Moorsele and the two naval squadrons in the coastal region remained in Flanders. To improve their strength, the naval squadrons were redeployed and part of I MLFA left Ghistelles for Beveren and II MLFA was divided between the Handzame and Ghistelles. However, the most effective reinforcement came with the arrival of a new fighter unit: Jagdstaffel 8, operating from

the Rumbeke airfield – but three aerodromes, Ghits, Menin-Coucou and Menin Halluin remained unmanned.

At the end of 1916 the battles of Verdun and the Somme came to an end, with a total loss of life of almost two million men.

The Coming of the Jastas

In autumn 1916 the Fourth Army in Flanders received its first *Jagdstaffeln* or Jastas (fighter squadrons), which would become the scourge of Allied airmen until the end of the war.

During the Battle of the Somme the Allies gained air superiority, and the German deployment of bomber squadrons as fighter units proved a costly failure. The German command had to react, and in August 1916, when German aerial strength was at it lowest, it was time for change. The first change was the creation of the post of *Inspektor der Fliegertruppen* or 'Idflieg' to control the technical organisation of the air force. This role was given to Major Siegert, former chief of the BAO. The second was the formation in August of permanent fighter squadrons equipped with new D-type fighter aircraft – the *Jagdstaffeln* or literally 'hunting squadrons'.

The task of these newly-formed squadrons was to intercept and destroy the enemy fighter aircraft and prevent Allied reconnaissance and army co-operation planes from doing their job, so securing safe airspace for their own reconnaissance planes.

The famous ace Oswald Boelcke, the father of the German fighter squadrons, developed simple rules for engagement
These were his key rules:

1 *A Jagdstaffel pilot always tries to secure a good position before attacking. He has to climb before and during the approach in order to surprise the enemy from above, then dive on him from the rear when the moment to attack is at hand.*

2 *Try to place yourself between the sun and the enemy. This means the sun is in the enemy's eyes making it difficult for him to see you and impossible for him to shoot with any accuracy.*

3 *Do not fire your machine-guns until the enemy is within range and you have him squarely within your sights.*

Halberstadt DI at Handzame. Two prototypes were tested and they performed well, which resulted in the commissioning of the Halberstadt DII, first produced in spring 1916. This was the preferred aircraft of the pilots of the early Jagdstaffeln until the Albatros DI became available (own collection).

4 Attack when the enemy least expects it or when he is preoccupied with other duties such as observation, photography, or bombing.

5 Never turn your back and try to run away from an enemy fighter. If you are surprised by an attack on your tail, make a turn and attack the enemy with your guns.

6 Keep your eye on the enemy and do not let him deceive you with tricks. If your adversary appears damaged, follow him down until he crashes to be sure he is not feigning damage.

7 Don't do anything rash or foolish. The Jagdstaffel must fight as a unit with close teamwork between all pilots. The signals of its leaders must always be obeyed.

In mid-September 1916 the first Jagdstaffel – shortened to Jasta – joined the Fourth Army, and Jasta 8 was stationed at Rumbeke, the former home of FFA 6. Hauptmann Gustav Stenzel took command, and it was a post he held until his death on 28 July 1917. At first the squadron had just six pilots, equipped with the new Albatros DII, but the impact of this fighting unit soon became apparent, as during the last three months of 1916 it claimed some ten victories – twice as many as the previous nine months' score of the units attached to the Fourth Army.

The success of the Jastas during 1916 can be attributed largely to the exceptionally high level of training for the fighter pilots and their advanced equipment – they performed better and were more heavily armed then their Allied counterparts.

In the last days of October 1916 a second German fighter unit arrived in Flanders. Jasta 18, commanded by Oberleutnant Heino von Grieffenhagen, and moved into Flugplatz Halluin, the former airfield of AFA 102B in the suburbs of Menin. At first the squadron had only four pilots, three of whom came from Jasta 8, but by the end of 1916 that number had increased to nine. The unit became operational on 11 January 1917 and recorded its first victory on 23 January, when Leutnant Walter von Bülow-Bothkamp shot down a British Sopwith 1 1/2 Strutter near Gheluvelt. The German air force had finally cut its teeth.

The Naval Corps Under Fire

The Allies made concentrated attacks on the harbours, workshops and aerodromes held by the German Naval Corps, by far the most far severe of which was launched at dawn on 20 March. A force of 44 aircraft – ten French bombers and five fighters, eight British bombers and five fighters and 11 Belgian bombers and five fighters – took off to bomb Mariakerke airfield, dropping a total of 111 bombs, while seven British seaplanes

No.	Date	Pilot	Victim	Location
1	1 October	Alfred Ulmer	Belgian balloon	Oost-Vleteren
2	16 October	Alfred Ulmer	Morane BB	Ennetières (France)
3	21 October	Weichel (FA 40)	Balloon	Nieppe (France)
4	22 October	Alfred Träger	DH2	Polygon Wood
5	14 November	Walter Göttsch (FA 33)	Belgian balloon	Oost-Vleteren
6	16 November	Peter Glasmacher	FE2b	West of Ypres
7	17 November	Wilhelm Seitz	FE2d	Not confirmed
8	17 November	Walter Göttsch	DH2	South west Ypres
9	26 December	Alfred Ulmer	Nieuport XII	Hooge

Albatros DII at the Jastaschule (fighter flying school) at Valenciennes in France. This was one of the first aircraft to have a radiator in the centre section of the upper wing (Collection Lawson USA).

dropped twenty-eight 30-kg/65-lb bombs on the seaplane base at Zeebruges.

In response, the Germans bombed the harbour of Dunkirk day and night from 19 to 22 May 1916, dropping a total of 372 bombs on the town, killing 32 people and wounding 89. Two German bomber units, comprising some 70 planes, took part in these attacks, for the loss of just two aircraft.

Towards the end of May the Allies made further bombing raids against German coastal airfields at Ghistelles on 19 April, Mariakerke on 23 and 24 April, and 5 and 21 May – but they still could not neutralise the German air threat in the region.

The German Naval Corps had established a strong squadron flying seaplane patrols from Zeebruges and, with the number of aircraft increasing from 12 in January to 28 in December, the Zeebruges squadron was a constant threat over the southern reaches of the North Sea.

During 1916 most seaplanes were fitted with wireless telegraphy equipment, in addition to the two pigeons they carried – but they now only resorted to these birds only when the new technology failed.

In the course of operations, some pilots from the Zeebruges seaplane base became fighter aces. In the period between May and September, Leutnant zur See Bönisch downed six enemy aircraft, but it was pilot Oberflugmeister Karl Meyer who notched up the top score with seven victories between July and October 1916.

In August single-seater seaplanes were introduced, and the corps was better fitted for its fighter role. The new aircraft were armed with a forward-firing synchronised machine-gun which shot through the propeller, and on 7 September Karl Meyer in Rumpler 6B1, No 751 forced an Allied Caudron to land on the water near Ostend.

Posing a constant threat to the Allied war effort, the seaplane base at Zeebruges became a key target and from 24 September, land-based Allied aircraft shot down six German seaplanes.

It was at the end of 1916 that three torpedo-planes arrived at Zeebruges. These two-engined seaplanes were designed with enough space between the floats to carry a torpedo. Two big new hangars and a third crane were installed to cater for these big water birds, which came under command of Leutnant zur See Becker.

In November the torpedo-planes scored their first victory, sinking a British cargo ship.

The weather improved on 9 November – winds force 2 on the Beaufort scale, west-north-west, height of the waves 1 to 2, with low clouds. The crews of the

Friedrichshafen FF33Ls at Zeebruges. Aircraft No 1247 is being lowered by crane into the water, the observer standing on the upper wing ready to release the hook. The seaman on the mole holds a rope to prevent the aircraft turning while suspended (Collection Plane).

torpedo-planes were delighted – at last they could demonstrate the power of their new aircraft. The torpedoes were checked and loaded under the aircraft, then the cranes lowered the torpedo-planes into the water.

The three torpedo-planes and their escort took off at 2 pm. Their mission was to disrupt the commercial traffic in the River Thames. Under cover of the dark clouds the little group avoided enemy interception and, because the sky lightened up near the British coast, the aircraft sought cover in banks of fog above the Downs.

3.45 pm: a cargo ship... a second one... a third... a whole convoy came into view. Zigzagging, the crews tried to get an overview of the whole convoy. There were fishing boats and a torpedo-boat protected the cargo ships.

They closed in fast on their prey. At 3.49 pm the attack began and the torpedo-planes flew straight on to their target – the last of the steamers. One by one they launched their torpedoes, then the aircraft made a sharp turn while their observers tracked the white trails of their missiles. Then suddenly, two explosions. Two rising columns of water showed the points of impact. Slowly the ship capsized and disappeared into the waves. The escorting craft opened fire without result.

4.45 pm: all seaplanes came home safely. The commander reported that his torpedoes had sunk a 2,000-tonne steamship.

Meanwhile, a central workshop was under construction in the centre of the picturesque village of Lissewege, a couple of miles from the Zeebruges Mole, to provide the seaplane base with every support facility from repairing damaged aircraft to assembling newly-arrived seaplanes. Near the railway station, in the garden of the public school, there was a water-tower, a small storeroom, an electric powerplant, a forge for aluminium, iron and copper, a few workshops, and a bathhouse. The Zeebruges seaplane base would never be prevented from operating due to lack of infrastructure or parts.

The two land-based naval squadrons continued operations through 1916. I MLFA at Mariakerke, under command of Leutnant der Reserve Soltenborn, operated with a dozen crews, making reconnaissance and bombing sorties in two-seater Aviatik and Albatros aircraft.

The unit also flew artillery-ranging sorties for the formidable Tirpitz Battery which, situated in the dunes near Ostend, had to withstand continuous bombardment by Allied vessels. The battery's four 28-cm guns had a range of some 32 km/20 miles, so the Allies called in heavy bombardment to take out this major threat. Since the battery was adjacent to I MLFA's airfield, the unit was forced to leave Mariakerke, and they moved to Ghistelles on 22 July.

II MLFA was based further east at Neumunster, and flying AGO C1s and Fokkers they operated in a fighter role against enemy aircraft in the coastal region and as escort protecting I MLFA. Leutnant der Reserve Mettlich had nine pilots, five observers and 12 aircraft under his command, and as equipment was improved from mid-1916 onwards, Fokkers gradually replaced the AGO CIs.

With heavy fighting at the Somme and Verdun, the German Fourth Army sent squadrons to reinforce air operations in these hotspots, and almost all flying units left Flanders. In northern Flanders only the Naval Corps held on to all its air support. On 24 September II MLFA sent four aircraft to the previously abandoned airstrip of Handzame and four to Ghistelles, then on 6 October I MLFA was split into the *Südgruppe* (southern group) of five biplanes under the command of Oberleutnant Schmidt-Koppen at Beveren near Roulers, while the remainder stayed in Ghistelles and was redesignated as the *Nordgruppe* (northern group).

Finally, at the end of 1916, the Fourth Army's shortage of air support was relieved with the arrival of new single-seater and two-seater units, and on 13 December II MLFA had their full quota of aircraft back at Neumunster. The I MLFA Südgruppe moved to Handzame on 29 December and finally arrived back in Ghistelles at the start of 1917.

Kapitän zur See Herr, commander of the Air Service of the Naval Corps, was well aware of the weakness of his flying units. His report of 1 November 1916 summarises the shortages:

The Naval Corps has an insufficient number of land-based aeroplanes at its disposal. The front line that our two Landflieger-Abteilungen are tasked with defending is now doubled in length. In addition, Allied aerial activity has increased in the coastal area. I Marine Landflieger Abteilung is equipped with twelve C-type biplanes and Fokker D's. These Fokkers are used to escort the reconnaissance planes. II Marine Landflieger Abteilung has four Fokker biplanes (D-planes with a 100-hp engine) and a few remaining Fokker monoplanes, all with different engines (160 hp, 100 hp and 80 hp Gnome).

Today C-type aircraft can no longer carry out their duties without a decent fighter escort, which means we don't have enough fighter planes. The few fighters we have are used exclusively to protect the artillery observation planes – they are not available to protect observation balloons or to intercept enemy scouts.

The three LVGs with 220-hp engine and the 160-hp Rumpler carry out long-distance reconnaissance work. Only six Albatros aircraft are available to support the artillery, and to perform this task an artillery plane needs to be escorted by three fighters. It takes this flying group two or three hours to range the artillery fire of two batteries. If they have to range targets for four batteries, the crews are airborne for more than five hours. Even the few single-seaters of I and II MLFA are completely outclassed. One of our Fokkers is a pre-war model and can no longer be used as a fighter.

The enemy has complete aerial superiority in the Naval Corps area and possesses technically superior fighter aircraft, therefore the need for 12 modern fighter planes for the Marine Corps is paramount.

Signed: Herr.

A nosed-over AGO CII at Neumunster – take-off and landing problems were common for these heavy machines on the soggy airfield. The AGOs of II Marine Landflieger-Abteilung were all given pet names: Pupchen (puppet), Hexe (witch) and Schneewitchen (Snow White) (own collection).

From August 1916 the Allies had undisputed air superiority over the coastal region – a situation that would last until the end of 1916, when German naval squadrons were supplied with better aircraft. Now, newly equipped with Halberstadt fighters, the Naval Corps was able to transform II MLFA at Neumunster into a small fighter squadron of about eight aircraft – the *Marine Einsitzer Kommando* (Naval Single-seater Commando) under the command of Obertleutnant zur See Von Santen. This unit later became the nucleus of the formidable *Marine Feldjagdstaffeln* (naval fighter section).

The French ace Guynemer with his Spad. He was shot down over the Ypres Salient on 11 September 1917 shortly after this picture was taken (own collection).

1917

New Personnel

On 8 October 1916 Generalleutnant Ernst von Hoeppner was appointed *Kommandierende General der Luftstreitkräfte* (Commanding General of the Air Force), which was abbreviated to Kogenluft. Von Hoeppner had almost complete power over air strategy, consulting only with the Chief of the General Staff of the Armies in the Field before ordering any action.

Oberstleutnant Thomson became Chief of the General Staff of Kogenluft. All the flying formations, except the Naval Air Service and the Bavarian units, came under the Kogenluft, so creating a united German Air Force.

The flying groups were now part of the individual armies themselves and no longer came under the command of the Army Corps Headquarters. Each army appointed a *Kommandeur der Flieger* (Chief of the Air Force), abbreviated to Kofl, and because most armies were split into a number of army groups, each of these had a *Gruppenführer der Flieger* (Group leader of the flying units, abbreviated to Grufl). This was an officer attached to Corps Headquarters responsible for the flying units assigned to the corps.

Hierarchy	New Rank
German Army	Kogenluft
Army	Kofl
Army Group	Grufl

The German Fourth Army appointed the following commanders:

Kofl	Date
Hauptmann Otto Bufe	October (?) 1916 - July 1917
Hauptmann Hellmuth Wilberg	July 1917 - end of war

During winter 1916 - 1917 the Fourth Army was re-organised into five groups, which were deployed along the front line from north to south: Gruppe Nord, Gruppe Dixmude, Gruppe Ypres, Gruppe Wijtschate and Gruppe Lille. This last group was transferred from the Sixth Army to the Fourth Army to provide better cover on the Ypres Salient.

The number of flying units increased and they were completely re-organised, with almost all squadrons being renamed, and now, better equipped and with more skilled and experienced personnel they were prepared to take on their duties.

The Jastas' main role remained aerial fighting – to hunt down and destroy enemy aircraft so that their own army co-operation units could work safely – and now they were constantly being re-equipped with improved fighter aircraft. They were also increasing in

The Pour le Mérite, known informally as the Blue Max, was the Kingdom of Prussia's highest order of merit. The last new member admitted to this class of the order was flying ace Theo Osterkamp, on 2 September, 1918.

strength, and during the first months of 1917 the number of Jastas rose from nine to 36.

The number of KAGOHLs was reduced to just three, which were equipped with twin-engined aircraft of the G (Grossflugzeug) category, and tasked with flying long-range bombing raids deep behind Allied lines and against targets in southern England.

The dismantled KAGOHLs reformed into 30 *Schutzstaffeln* (protection squadrons) or Schustas, whose duty was to escort and protect the two-seaters of the FAs.

In January 1917, 48 of the existing FFAs were re-named Flieger-Abteilungen; the remainder became Flieger-Abteilung (A). The difference was that the FAs flew long-distance reconnaissance sorties, while the FA (A)s worked in liaison with the artillery – the aim was to attach one such unit to each division.

Taking advantage of the calm period during winter 1916 -1917, the Kogenluft redeployed his aerial resources, sending an increasing number of units to the Fourth Army in Flanders, which had lacked adequate air support during the second half of 1916. In December 1916 the Fourth Army had only five flying units: I Marine Flieger-Abteilung, II Marine Flieger-Abteilung, Flieger-Abteilung 33, Jastas 8 and 18, and Flieger-Abteilung (A) 250, the last of which had only arrived at Coucou during November.

In January these five were reinforced by three new units: FA 3 at Bisseghem, FA 19 at Handzame and FA (A) 294 at Herseaux near Mouscron, which gave the Fourth Army air support as follows:

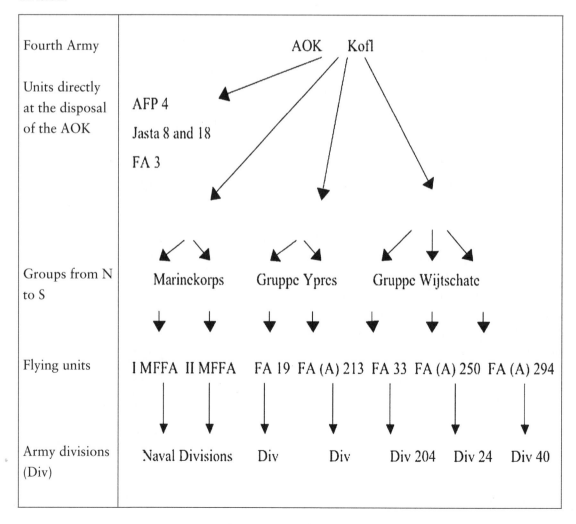

New aircraft
arrive at Armee
Flugpark IV (AFP
4) at Ghent. It
was the task
of the AFP to
keep the flying
units supplied
with updated
equipment and
skilled personnel
(collection
Raven).

Towards the end of the Battle of Verdun the FAs were given the additional duty of co-operating with the infantry and maintaining communication between the front line and the Army Headquarters.

During the first months of 1917 the Germans took the first steps to create what became known as *Infanteriefliegern* (Infantry Contact Patrols) – a taxing operation that called for rigorous training for both the aircrews and ground troops. Specially trained aircrews would fly over the trenches at low altitude and provide information to headquarters regarding the direction of the enemy attacks, the positions of their own front-line troops and what support those troops needed.

The Commander of the Fourth Army, Duke Albrecht von Württemberg, set great store by the benefits of close co-operation between the air force and the troops on the ground, and he ensured that men from each FA were given specialised contact patrol training. One of these trained men's first duties was to instruct the infantry in this new style of operating, and they visited the regiments giving lectures accompanied by slides. In return, infantry officers were invited to visit the airfields so they could see the potential of air support, and joint training exercises were carried out to hone their skills.

FAs 33 and (A) 294 spent February and March 1917 introducing the new system to their group, Gruppe Wijtschate. The infantrymen learned how to communicate with the aircrews by signalling-lamps, magnesium torches or spreading out strips of

A German aircraft
on contact patrol
– the infantry
shows its position
by laying out
white sheets,
sending up Very
lights and by
waving their arms
(own drawing).

white cloth, and were trained in the different signals sent by the aircrew to the ground – assorted colours of Very light, signalling-lamps, message-bags and sounding the klaxon.

In February the Fourth Army was reinforced by five more units: Jastas 27 and 28, the Marine Feldjagdstaffel and FA 6 (Group Wijtschate) and FA (A) 224 (Group Ypres). Of these, only the two reconnaissance units had prior experience – the three fighter squadrons consisted of a small nucleus of pilots who made their first combat sorties on 15 February (Jasta 27), 2 April (Jasta 28) and the first of May (Marine Feldjagdstaffel).

The following is an excerpt from the war diary of Jasta 27:

Two aircraft, with pilots and mechanics, are to be sent to Jasta 27 by both Jasta 8 and 18. In addition AFP 4, Ghent, will supply three aircraft, and the squadron commander, with his own aircraft, will bring the total number of aircraft assigned to this new squadron to eight. Our home airfield will be at Ghistelles. The first mobilisation for Jastas 27 and 31 is to be 5 February 1917, while that of Jasta 29 will be 13 February. The squadron commander is Leutnant von Keudell.

A great loss to the squadron, von Keudell was shot down during his first flight over the front on 15 February:

Over Boezinge at 5.40 pm, Leutnant von Keudell shot down a Nieuport, his 12th victory and the squadron's first. Unfortunately von Keudell himself crashed behind enemy lines after combat and was killed.

Leutnant Träger described the crash:

Leutnant von Keudell took off leading a formation of three Albatros DIIIs and

one DI. Due to engine trouble, the DI had to return home. East of Boezinge they gave chase to an enemy aircraft, but without success. Suddenly von Keudell dived on to an enemy flying towards Vlamertinge. The accompanying aircraft could not follow and they lost sight of the plane. After circling the area without finding their leader, they returned to their airfield.

Confirmation of his death came some days later in a letter from the Red Cross:

To the relatives of the late Lieutenant Hans von Keudell, German Flying Corps,

I regret to inform you of the death in action of Lieutenant von Keudell on the 15th February. He was flying on the British side of the line when he encountered a British aircraft.

In the ensuing fight the German plane showed signs of being damaged, and it suddenly seemed to drop. Almost immediately it caught fire and crashed into the ground, nose first, about a thousand yards behind our line.

On examination it was found that Lieutenant von Keudell was already dead. He had been shot through the chest and had serious burns to his legs and thighs. He was conveyed to the mortuary and today, the 16th, we laid him to his last rest in the British Cemetery, with the full rites of the Church of England.

The grave of Leutnant von Keudell, Commander of Jasta 27. He was shot down and crashed on 15 February 1917 and was buried in Ferme Olivier Cemetery near Poperinghe (own collection).

With the deepest expressions of sympathy to all the relatives of a gallant foe.

N.B. A suitably inscribed cross will be erected over the grave with all haste.

FA 6, flying from Heule-Watermolen, became operational during April, and in the meantime, the Naval Corps was reinforced by a *Kampfeinsitzer Staffel* (single-seater fighter squadron) or Kest 8 at Neumunster, which belonged to the Army of the Kingdom of Württemberg.

The Kests were created to protect strategically important German cities, and by April 1917 nine such units were operational. However, through necessity, the home defence Kests 3, 5, 7 and 8 were moved to the Western Front to fill in and buy time while new Jastas were formed. Further south FA (A) 294 returned from its secondment to the Sixth Army, arriving by train at its new base at Herseaux. This artillery-spotting unit, under the command of Hauptmann Kogler, flew for Divisions 24 and 204 of Group Wijtschate.

Armourers loading photographic plates, machine-gun and bullets in an ammunition drum on to a LVG CIV (Collection Raven).

May started with the arrival of two new units – FAs (A) 204 and 221, the latter of which flew from Bisseghem, west of Courtrai, for Group Ypres. By late May, as tension at the front rose, an avalanche of new units arrived in Flanders.

A Diabolical Plan

Early in 1917 the British were preparing an important strategic move in Flanders – a breakthrough in the Ypres Salient to capture the North Sea ports of Ostend and Zeebruges where the increasingly predatory German submarines were berthed.

However, the military situation in Flanders was not favourable for an Allied offensive. The Germans held the high ground around the Ypres Salient, making a British breakthrough almost impossible.

To address this problem the British High Command adopted a new strategy to blow up the German positions using underground mines. The British began digging tunnels towards the German lines and in May they had completed 19 tunnels that led directly under the German troop positions between Hill 60 and Ploegsteert Forest, and filled them with 450,000 kg/1 million lb of high explosive.

Personnel of Armee Flugpark 4 at Ghent, with their huge aircraft camera with a focal length of 120 cm. A number of photographic glass plates are laid out on the ground (Collection Raven).

German aircrews detected the Allied build-up almost immediately and reported an increased number of army camps, batteries, vehicles and trenches. It wasn't long before it became evident that the British were preparing to launch an offensive between Hill 60 and the Ypres-Comines canal. The German command hoped that they could gather vital information about the British intentions by means of a series of minor counter-attacks. One of these attacks took place soon after daybreak on 24 March 1917. A reinforced regiment stormed the British trenches, blowing up five tunnel entrances and capturing many troops. High in the sky, two aircraft of FA (A) 250 called in artillery fire while fighters of Jasta 18 protected the whole operation. An LVG aircraft of FA 33, which was photographing the operation from high altitude, was shot down. Leutnant Knoll of regiment 313 witnessed the event – the third loss by FA 33 that month – and made the following report:

At around 10.45 am the plane whirled down and crashed just before the line of our trenches. The plane was stuck with its engine submerged in the mud of a water-filled bomb-crater. Attempts to save the crew were very dangerous but some of our men managed to reach the wreck. They found the observer dead and the pilot still alive but trapped under the fuselage. Heavy shelling obliged our men to return to their trenches.

At 2.15 pm Leutnant Vogt and four of his men made another attempt to rescue the pilot. They managed to free him from his aircraft and carried him to the nearest road and on to a first-aid post. He had broken his kneecap and lost a finger.

Today we were able to recover the body of the observer Leutnant Reichle, but in the meantime the plane had been hit several times and only the tail was

still visible – the engine and cockpit had disappeared into the mud.

We did not find the camera – observer Reichle had most probably lost it after he was hit by shrapnel.

Despite this German operation, the British threat remained and German aircrews continued to return alarming reports:

Photo-reconnaissance revealed an exceptional build-up of enemy camps in front of our Ypres, Wijtschate and Lille Groups. They are mostly located west of Vlamertinge, Ouderdom, Clytte, Loker, and Dranouter. All camps are full of troops, with large numbers of guns and there is a lot of traffic on the roads and through the railway stations.

There is also an increase in the number of railway lines between Ypres and Armentières. Photographic and visual reconnaissance confirms a growing number of guns in front of the Ypres and Wijtschate groups and the northern part of Group Lille. Particularly noteworthy are the many covered positions between the village of Wulvergem and Zillebeke Lake. The enemy has even extended their trenches west of Messines and in the northern part of the Group Wijtschate.

Artillery-planes observed major explosions when enemy artillery positions were hit by our guns – which suggests the presence of large quantities of explosives and ammunition.

FAs 6, 19, 33, (A) 204, 213, 221, 227, 250, 294 and I and II Marine Feldflieger Abteilung located 236 enemy batteries, of which 65 were new. Our guns opened fire on 37 of these enemy positions.

Meanwhile Allied aerial activity has grown to dangerous levels. By day they are mostly occupied helping their artillery, but at night they carry out bombing raids deep inside our territory.

This increasing Allied activity compelled the German air force to concentrate on bombing enemy positions and intercepting intruding enemy aircraft. Between 26 May and 1 June they were engaged in 128 dogfights, but the Germans notched up only three 'kills': on 27 May Offizier-Stellvertreter Müller of Jasta 28 brought down a Sopwith east of Ypres and Leutnant Strähle of Jasta 18 a BE near Armentières, then on 1 June a FE single-seater was downed near Houthem. Germany suffered one loss when Unteroffizier Hertel of Jasta 10 was severely injured in a crash.

By the end of May the number of flying units had almost doubled – 13 new units were quickly brought in to support the Fourth Army: FAs 7 and 8, (A) 227, 231, 258, 293, Jastas 4, 10, 20, Kastas 1 and 23 and Schustas 19 and 24B.

The Allied Attack

On 7 June at 3.10 am, the Allies simultaneously detonated the high explosive mines under the German positions. The results were beyond belief. The ridge between Messines and Hill 60 was completely blown apart. Entire German battalions were buried alive and the explosion was heard as far away as London and Paris. With the support of artillery fire, gas and low flying aircraft the British stormed the German trenches.

At 3.45 am the first German aircrews appeared over the site and saw an apocalyptic scene. Craters some 60 m/65 yd wide had replaced the German trenches. Fire and smoke filled the sky and obscured the first light of day. Hundreds of flashes from the firing batteries illuminated the darkness. Hauptmann Freiherr von Pechmann, of

A captured British Spad SVII repainted in German colours and an Albatros CX at Moorsele airfield. The Spad was brought down on 18 June 1917 (collection Haerynck Belgium).

The wreckage of a triplane, N6306, of Naval 10 of the RNAS, near St-Katherine (Heule-Lendelede). It was brought down on 24 June 1917 by Leutnant Groos of Jasta 11; the pilot, Holcroft MIA, was made a prisoner of war (Collection Plane).

FA 33, was one of the first German aerial observers to arrive. He described the inferno below:

Far away, above the horizon, more than 30 Allied observation balloons, protected by swarms of fighter planes, filled the sky. On Hill 60, two enormous craters had opened up. In our foremost lines there was no sign of life. In the second line of trenches our infantrymen signalled to me by firing Very lights, and near Messines our troops spread white sheets on the ground when we flew over.

The German aircrews found it hard to locate the Allied batteries and to stay in contact with their own ground troops and it wasn't until the evening of the first day that they established the position of the front line.

FA (A) 221 flew in support of 119th Division and on 7 June reported:

Nine contact patrol flights (three involving aerial combat) and one escort flight (also involving combat). During the Horn-Classen crew's contact patrol,

Horn was injured by anti-aircraft fire. All planes returned safely. Leutnant Horn and Unteroffizier Donhauser were sent to the hospital.

It was also very difficult for the German crews to remain above their own trenches as they came under constant attack. The Jastas were sent as support to protect the reconnaissance planes and the sky was filled with dogfights. Germany claimed ten Allied aircraft shot down, but they still could not establish aerial supremacy above the lines where hundreds of aircraft were duelling.

Flying low, at 300 – 600 m/900 – 1,800 ft above the trenches, the FAs experienced a lot of problems in maintaining contact with their troops in the battle zone and in locating enemy positions, and during the first days the contact patrol flights yielded poor results. Very often the infantrymen were frightened of drawing enemy attention and did not spread out their white sheets. However, by mid-June ground-to-air communication had improved and was working almost perfectly.

German reconnaissance crews were further hampered by the fact that the sky was full of anti-aircraft fire, infantry fire and Allied fighter planes, so the German command responded by calling in every available Jasta and Schusta plane. Helped by these reinforcements, the FAs returned to their vital role directing the artillery and reporting the enemy advances, but despite this the British took Messines Ridge on 11 June.

In the first week of the offensive some 200 aerial combats took place, during which 22 Allied and three German planes were shot down, and some 7,300 German troops were taken prisoner. The British suffered only 'minor' casualties with 25,000 killed.

The Allied offensive took the German High Command completely by surprise and they immediately sent massive reinforcements into Flanders, including 27 flying units, with Group Ypres in particular receiving additional aircraft. The German High Command also decided to send the newly-formed elite fighter group, Jagdgeschwader I, under the command of Manfred von Richthofen, to the Ypres Salient.

The Arrival of Jagdgeschwader I

During the first half of 1917 the German air force was increasingly outnumbered by their Allied counterparts, and size of a *Jagdstaffel* (fighter squadron) was smaller than that of a comparable British or French squadron, so the Kofl commanders of some German armies amalgamated their fighter squadrons into larger groups.

At the end of June, the first organised group of Jastas – numbers 4, 6, 10 and 11 – became *Jagdgeschwader I* (JG I) under the command of Germany's most successful ace, Manfred von Richthofen,

General Headquarters, 26 June 1917. By order of the Chief of General Staff of the Army in the Field, as of 23 June – Ic Nr 5834-1 – Jastas 4, 6, 10 and 11 will become Jagdgeschwader I. This squadron is an independent unit and will be tasked with gaining and maintaining aerial supremacy in certain war zones. Signed: Chief of General Staff, Thomsen

Ypres

Zillebeke

Gheluveld

Hill 60

FA 33

Exploded British Mines

Frontline

Zandvoorde

FA (A) 250

Hollebeke

FA 8

Tenbrielen

FA (A) 294

Houthem

Wytschate

JS 4

FA 6

Comines

SS 24B

River Lys

Messines

Warneton

Unit flying for a division

Unit flying for an army group

German aerial strength in Group Wijtschate on the eve of the Allied breakthrough on 7 June 1917.

Kogenluft 64683 Fl II (27.6.1917): the airfields to the south west of Courtrai are requisitioned to bring together the four Jastas in one aerodrome. They are the airfields of Marke, Marckebeke and Bisseghem. The squadrons must be ready for action on 2 July.

On 2 July von Richthofen's JG I was indeed ready in its new bases. Oberleutnant Bodenschatz and Leutnant Kreft served as adjutant and technical officer respectively, and they set up headquarters in the Château de Béthune near Marckebeke airfield. Von Richthofen appointed Leutnant Kurt Wolff leader of Jasta 11, Oberleutnant Kurt-Bertram Rittmeister von Doering leader of Jasta 4, Oberleutnant Eduard Ritter von Dostler in charge of Jasta 6 and Oberleutnant Ernst Freiherr von Althaus leading Jasta 10. Jastas 11 and 4 were based at Marckebeke, while Jasta 6 flew from Bisseghem and Jasta 10 from Marke.

The average age of the pilots was 22, but the commanders were some three to four year older. Commander Rittmeister Manfred Freiherr von Richthofen was born the son of a rich *Junker* (a large landowner) on 2 May 1892 in Scheidwitz, a Polish town near Breslau. He started his military career at the age of 17 and became a lieutenant in the First Uhlanen (Cavalry) Regiment. In the first months of the war he saw action on the Eastern Front but in May 1915 he transferred to the air service where he became an observer. After pilot training at the beginning of 1916 he joined KG 2 in the Verdun sector, scoring his first confirmed victory on 17 September 1916, serving with Jasta 2. He had scored 80 victories when he was finally shot down on 21 April 1918. He remained the greatest of the German aces and the pilot with the highest score throughout the war.

The Red Baron (he got this name because his planes were mostly red) scored seven victories over the Belgian part of Flanders (see below).

However, von Richthofen was not the highest scoring German pilot in the Flanders campaign – Werner Voss notched up 14 victories, Bongartz of Jasta 36, 23 and Jacobs of Jasta 7 an extraordinary 44.

Von Richthofen's younger brother Lothar (1894 - 1922) was also a successful fighter pilot, and serving with Jasta 11, notched up 40 victories – but only one of these in Flanders.

After the war, Adjutant Karl Bodenschatz wrote an acclaimed book on the exploits of JG I, *Jagd in Flanderns Himmel –*

Date	Aircraft shot down	Place	number of win
18 June 1917	RE 8 (A4290) of 9 Squadron RFC (2 KIA)	North of Ypres	53
23 June 1917	Spad VII 23 Sq (?)	North of Ypres	54
24 June 1917	DH 4 (A7473) of 57 Squadron RFC (2KIA)	Beselare (Keibergmolen)	55
25 June 1917	RE 8 (A3847) of 53 Squadron RFC (2 KIA*)	Le Bizet	56
16 August 1917	Nieuport XXIII (A6611) of 29 Squadron RFC (1 KIA**)	South-west of Houthulst Forest	58
26 August 1917	Spad VII (B3492) of 19 Squadron RFC: (1 KIA)	Between Poelkapelle and Langemark	59
2 September 1917	RE 8 (B782) of 6 Squadron RFC (1 POW and 1 KIA***)	North-west of Zonnebeke)	60
J A Power-Clutterbuck is buried in Ploegsteert (Strand Military Cemetery)			
** *W H T Williams and *** W Kember are buried in Harlebeke New British Cemetery*			

Manfred von Richthofen's Albatros D V, No 1177/17 after his crash landing near Wervicq-Sud, just inside the French border. Von Richthofen was shot in the head but survived to return to his comrades of JG I some two weeks later (own collection).

Von Richthofen photographed during his convalescence with fellow officers at Marckebeke Château (own collection).

aus den zechszehn Kampfmonaten des Jagdgeschwaders Freiherr von Richthofen (Combat in the sky of Flanders – from Richthofen's JG I's sixteen months in action). An important document in the history of JG I, the book was published in 1935 and became a bestseller in Hitler's Germany.

When all the squadrons are at the aerodrome you could easily distinguish the 12 aircraft of each commander. There are only two aircraft – the Albatros DV and the Pfalz D III. The whole squadron is very colourful – all the aircraft of Jasta 11, von Richthofen's unit, are painted red, those of Jasta 10 are yellow, Jasta 4 has a single black spiral over the standard colour of its fuselage, and Jasta 6 has black and white zebra stripes on the tailplanes.

German troops awaiting the arrival of the Kaiser Wilhelm II. The photo shows (1) Manfred von Richthofen with Pour La Mérite, (2) Oberleutnant von Pechmann, (3) Oberleutnant Dostler, also with PLM, two days before his death, (4) Leutnant Bongartz and (5) unknown (collection Nielebock Germany).

*German laurelled soldiers
saluting the German emperor
at Machelen aan de Leie or
St-Denijs-Westrem, 19 August
1917. The emperor pays
special attention to his top-ace:
Manfred von Richthofen, his
head still bandaged after his
accident of 6 July 1917.*

No two aircraft were painted exactly the same – all the German fighter pilots had their personal colours, stripes and markings, which made it easy for them to recognise each other during aerial combat. The aggressive colours also gave the German pilots a psychological advantage, making their aircraft look especially intimidating to the enemy.

Almost immediately, JG I made its mark. Operational from 5 July, its pilots scored 69 victories during the first month – however, five pilots were killed and five more wounded. Among the wounded was Manfred von Richthofen, who suffered a serious gunshot wound to the head on 6 July and only just managed to land safely in Wervicq-Sud – but on 25 July he was back in command of JG I.

During July 1917 Oberleutnant Dostler, CO of Jasta 6, was the most successful member of JG I, with nine victories. A German officer witnessed one of his engagements:

It was summertime, shortly before the start of the Third Battle of Ypres. The weather was fine and favourable to the British intruders. They penetrated our airspace with groups of up to 20 aircraft, looking for targets to bomb or locations to photograph. Our fighter planes were in action from dawn to dusk, chasing these intruders and they experienced great difficulty fighting these close-flying formations.

On one particular day I was driving through the little town of Ingelmunster and from two or three plumes of smoke I deduced that an Allied bombardment was still in progress. I ordered my driver to get out of the danger area as fast as possible. As we passed the railway station, I saw that it was packed with materiel, horses and troops, and quickly realised that this would be a prime target for enemy bombers. We laid up some

500 m from the station and waited. After a short time, high in the sky we saw six British aircraft. One by one they left the formation and bombed the railway station – but no bombs hit the target. Suddenly the planes dispersed. We could clearly hear the noise of machine-guns and two of our Albatros fighters fell like eagles on to the British aircraft.

After only the first few shots one Englishman was shot down. He went down in a steep spin and caught fire, then the upper wing broke off. Some while later we saw one of the crew falling out of the plane, which crashed to the ground in flames. Meanwhile, the German fighter attacked a second target. He closed in from behind and after a few shots the plane went down in flames.

Now the German pilot looked for his next target. One after another the British were attacked and shot down to the sound of loud applause from the troops on the ground.

Some days later we heard that Leutnant Adam and the Bavarian, Oberleutnant Dostler, were the two victors.

From mid-August, inspired by the success of JG I, Hauptmann Wilberg, Kogenluft of the Fourth Army decided to create more Jasta groups, but unlike JG 1 these were not permanent and the personnel often changed. All the same, these large groups of fighters were able to wrest back aerial supremacy during the course of the Third Battle of Ypres.

The Naval Flyers Get Their Teeth

The air service of the Naval Corps in Flanders increased in strength during the last two years of the war, becoming a smaller copy of the *Fliegertruppen* (flying troops) of the German Army.

At the end of 1916, II MLFA was disbanded, but some of its remnants formed

the nucleus of a new naval squadron whose main role was as a fighter unit, intercepting and destroying enemy aircraft. The pilots would learn their fighting skills under the command of Leutnant zur See Sachsenberg – who already had half a year's fighter experience in Fokker E IIIs.

Equipped with one Albatros C I (No LF 125) and two modern Halberstadt fighters (a DIII, No 394/16 and a DV, No 406/16) the *Marine Feldjagdstaffel* (Naval Land Fighter Squadron) or Marine Jasta came into being on 1 February, and was very soon recording successes with Vizeflugmeister Wirtz scoring the first victory on 7 February. At first the unit operated from Neumunster, then moved on 1 April to a new location at Aartrijke, near the rest home and monastery. This airfield was a long way inland – 32 km/20 miles into the Fourth Army's sector.

A *Kommando des Luftfahrtwesens des Marinekorps* (Naval Corps Air Service Commando), under command of Kapitän zur See Stubenrauch, was established at the headquarters in Bruges to co-ordinate the growing number of flying units. By the end of the war this commando comprised four sections: the *Seeflugwesen*, the *Feldflugwesen*, the *Küstenartillerieflieger* and the *Marinejagdgeschwader* (respectively the flying seaplanes, field aviation, coastal artillery support and marine fighters).

The seaplanes of the *Seeflugwesen* were put under the *Kommandeur der Luftseefront* (Commander of the Coastal Front) Tschirschky und Bogendorf, who until that point had been commander at Zeebruges, and was replaced there by *Oberleutnant der Reserve der Marine Artillerie* (Senior Lieutenant of the Reserve, Naval Artillery) Friedrich Christiansen on 15 September 1917.

Zeebruges was Germany's most important seaplane base throughout the war, and in February 1917 it was home to 53 aircraft, 43 pilots and observers and some 300 ground personnel. The single- and two-seater seaplanes carried out patrols over the sea and along the coasts of England, France, Belgium and Holland, monitored commercial maritime traffic, protected the minelayers and torpedo-boats, harried Allied aircraft and shipping and gave support to the coastal artillery.

In March 1917, II *Torpedostaffel* (torpedo squadron – *II T-Staffel*), a specialised torpedo squadron, arrived at Zeebruges. The first successful attack by the unit occurred on 17 April 1917, as Leutnant Freude and Flugmaat Berhoff sank a dredger off the English coast. In September it was joined by I T-Staffel, whose first victory was on 9 September:

2.10 pm – fine weather. Three torpedo-planes took off: 995 (Leutnant zur See Stinsky, Flugmatrose Neuerburg), 1211 (Schürer-Mertens) and 1213 (Hübrich-Rowehl). Three single-seaters of the C-Staffel flew as escort. The group

headed north-west and sank a 500-tonne steamship with just two hits. At 4.55 pm all aircraft arrived home.

By the end of 1916, a second seaplane base had been built in the harbour basin at Ostend. *Flandern II* was under the command of Kapitänleutnant Bücker and became operational during March 1917, with four aircraft, five pilots and 100 ground crew. On 14 March the unit scored its first victory – a French flying boat. Equipped with single-seaters fighters, the second Flanders fighter squadron scored four more victories during April and gradually took on the same duties as *Flandern I* (the first Flanders seaplane unit) at Zeebruges. The Ostend-based flyers covered the Ostend-Margate-Thames estuary area and the Zeebruges squadron covered the area further north.

Long-range reconnaissance over land in the Nieuport and Dixmude area was carried out by two *Marinefeldflieger Abteilungen*

(German naval aerial reconnaissance units) or MFFA, the first of which, under Leutnant der Reserve Treischke, was formed on 21 January 1917, seconding pilots and aircraft from the Nordgruppe of the disbanded I MLFA. During the first part of 1917 this squadron was based at Ghistelles, then on 16 June it moved to newly-built facilities at Vlisseghem, a small village east of Ostend, 8 km/5 miles from the coast.

An extract from the squadron's war diary describes a typical day on operations:

16 July 1917. During the day six aircraft took off – one carried out range-finding sorties for the artillery, and the others carried out a reconnaissance patrol. Thick cloud prevented us from providing good range information for the guns of 4 Batterie Fuss [Fourth Foot Artillery]. The crew could not see where the shells were exploding.

There was little traffic behind the front. We took some pictures of the sluices at Nieuport, but enemy aircraft thwarted all our attempts to penetrate above enemy territory. During aerial combat, one of two attacking Spads dived steeply away.

Summary of the day: six sorties, a total of five and three-quarter hours. Ammunition fired: 200 rounds and 30 tracers.

Later in January the southern group of I MLFA became II MFFA, and in spring the group transferred to the new aerodrome at Jabbeke, some 16 km/10 miles south-west of Bruges. On 22 August the squadron moved closer to Bruges, to Meetkerke.

These units used the same aircraft as the Fliegertruppen, and in July I MFFA had six two-seaters, five LVGs and one Rumpler. On 27 October the second squadron acquired a seventh plane – an armoured Junkers JI fighter.

In spring 1917 *Schutzstaffel* (protection or escort squadron) or Schusta came into operation. Their main role was to escort and protect aircraft which were providing support to the infantry and artillery, but they could also be used for short-range reconnaissance and artillery-spotting work. The first Schustas arrived with the Fourth Army in Flanders during May.

A *Marine Schutzstaffel* (naval escort squadron) was also formed at this time, which was seconded to I MFFA. The following is an extract from the squadron's war diary:

> 4 August 1917. Three aircraft dropped 12 25-lb bombs on enemy batteries east of Dixmude. Explosions were sighted. Thereafter they fired 1,500 rounds on Belgian trenches on the west bank of the River Yser, north of Nieuport, from a height of 250-300m/700 -1,000 ft.

The aircraft of Kest 8 were brought in to replace the naval fighters in the coastal region, but they were not a successful fighting squadron and stayed in Flanders for only a few months before returning to Germany to resume their original role – the protection of Germany's industrial areas.

A villager was unimpressed by the Marine Jasta in Aartrijke:

> 24 February. There is to be an airfield at the rest-home.
> 26 February. This morning 40 men arrived to work on the airfield. They are people from a neighbouring village.
> 26 March. The new airmen will be from the navy.
> 8 April. All trees that have been felled to clear the airfield are to be sold.
> 11 April. The airmen went to Ghent to buy towels, napkins and tablecloths (70 yards of tablecloth). The municipality has to pay the bill.
> Monday 16 April. The three first planes of the new unit arrived. It is prohibited for any inhabitants and

Albatros DVs and DIIIs of a Marine Jagdstaffel at Varsenare (Collection Plane).

especially children to wander on to the airfield.

19 April. The airmen have bought very expensive stoves. Again the municipality has to pay.

24 April. Everything quiet. Wirtz, the famous ace from our airfield, took off this morning and was shot down in the vicinity of Ypres.

25 April. Yesterday an aeroplane landed of the side of the airfield. The place is too small and is going to be expanded.

30 April. The airmen stole Mr Crivit's billiard table and have installed it in the rest-home.

Wednesday 9 May. A car arrived with the dead body and the wrecked aircraft of one of the airmen.

10 May. A big vehicle arrived with an anti-aircraft gun.

11 June. In the last four days four airmen have gone missing or been killed. Hurrah!

Thursday 11 September. The seamen from the rest-home have left the village. Farewell, monstrous thieves!

The aircraft which arrived on 16 April were the first Albatros D IIIs – the unit also had an older Albatros D II, which was used as a trainer.

The loss on 24 April was the unit's first, Vizefeldwebel Wirtz was killed in a mid-air collision with an allied plane over Beselare.

The Beach Party, July 1917

In the north-west corner of Belgium the River Yser forms a natural defensive barrier and during the war the Allies held only the area west of the river in this flat coastal region. In December 1914, French troops captured a small stronghold 3 km/2 miles long and just 250 m/274 yd wide on the east bank of the river in the dunes just north of Nieuport. By 1917 British troops had replaced the French in this area.

During the first half of 1917, German reconnaissance reported a build-up of Allied forces in the northern area of the Western Front, and it became clear to the German High Command that the enemy was massing for an invasion in Flanders, so it was vital to reinforce the Fourth Army holding the Flanders sector. The German command brought in new troops and almost emptied its arsenals to provide the Fourth Army with artillery, aircraft and ammunition. It also launched *Operation Strandfest* (Operation Beach-Party) to recover the small British stronghold on the east bank of Yser.

For the first time aircraft would play a major role in the Flanders conflict, and during late June every available German squadron was brought in and schooled in their role which was planned with the strategy of a chess-master. By July 1917 Germany had 24 squadrons in the region: I and II MFFAs, FA (A) 293, Schustas 1 and 29, the Marinefeldjagdstaffel, Jastas 17 and 20 and Kest 23 (from the Marine Corps), FAs 48B and (A) 231 and Schusta 16 (from Gruppe Dixmude – the northern sector of the Fourth Army, adjacent to the Marine Corps sector). Jastas 7 and 8 also took part and, last but not least, the four elite Jastas of JG I from Marke and Bisseghem, under command

An aerial view of the River Yser near Nieuport, taken by I Marine Feldflieger-Abteilung on August 19, 1917 at 3.45 pm from an altitude of 600 m/2,000 ft. From left to right (west to east): the Furnes and Koolhof canals, the Yser River, Nieuwendamme cove, the Plassendale Canal, the western waterway and flooded land. These canals converged into the strategically important Nieuport Canal, which was held by Belgian troops. In the background is the Yser Estuary (own collection).

Heavily damaged twin-engined AEG GIV of Kagohl I on its nose on Beveren airfield. The Roman character for the Kasta identication is visible on the fuselage. The left undercarriage is torn off. A portion of a rack with 25 lb. (10 kg) bombs is visible under the fuselage of the bomber.

of the Red Baron, and the six Kampfstaffeln of KG 1. (This last group left its base at Asq, north of Lille in France, and moved to Ghistelles.) An armada of some 200 aircraft was amassed in a small zone 16 km/10 miles wide, in preparation for the attack.

There was a danger that Allied reconnaissance aircraft and intelligence-gathering services might still uncover the German master-plan, and if the assault was to succeed, it had to achieve total surprise. The build-up was carefully hidden from Allied observers – all aerial activity in the region was carried out at low level and JG I's transfer from its airfields near Courtrai to Jabbeke was delayed until the last minute. The big bombers of KG I arrived at Ghistelles on 7 July and were quickly taxied into the hangars – they would not be needed until the night before the ground-attack when they would carry out bombing raids.

The day before the attack all artillery, aircraft and troops were in position and ready for action, however the weather posed a major problem. It had been raining cats and dogs for days and the High Command was forced to postpone the operation from 8 to 10 July.

The weather was still bad on 10 July, but despite adverse conditions, it was decided to go ahead. The assault began with a massive artillery barrage.

It was still dark when an aircraft of II MFFA took off to patrol deep inside Allied airspace. The crew were to report the arrival of any Allied reinforcements to headquarters – they would be relieved at 11 am and 5 pm. At 6 am two aircraft, one from I MFFA at Vlisseghem and one from FA (A) 293 at Ghistelles, took off for the front. Their role was to report on the impact of the previous days' bombardment on the British defences.

The plan went into action at 10 am with a massive artillery barrage, supported by artillery-spotting aircraft of FA (A) 231, I and II MFFAs and FA (A) 293. Using these aircraft in a new way, they took turns to fly over the fighting area, so that the German command had continual updates on the progress of the battle. It had been prearranged that there would be two short pauses in the artillery barrage to allow the reconnaissance planes to transmit their reports to the headquarters. Alternatively they could fly to one of two communication centres, marked with two big white crosses on the ground, and drop message-bags and read ground-signals.

This intensive use of aircraft proved very effective. Early in the afternoon crews of FA (A) 293 and I and II MFFAs reported the destruction of all footbridges across the Yser River – the British were now trapped in their positions on the east bank, with no way of retreating to join their main forces on the other side of the river. In addition, two aircraft of FA (A) 293 returned from daring forays deep inside Allied airspace and provided the German command with vital information and photographs, the latter showing very clearly the arrival of Allied reinforcements.

The heavy bombardment was the prelude to the infantry assault, and at 7.51 pm the ground attack began. Men of the 3rd Naval Infantry Division left their trenches and stormed the British positions. Four aircraft of KG I supported the ground troops by attacking the enemy from the air with machine-gun fire and hand grenades. High in the air, an infantry support aircraft of I MFFA followed the progress of the German advance and radioed reports back to headquarters, protected by two aircraft of Schusta 29.

To prevent a British counter-attack, the FAs bombarded the west bank, with two aircraft taking turns to overfly enemy positions for five minutes at a time. Every group made two sorties so the enemy was under heavy aerial bombardment for two hours.

At the same time, the heavy bombers of KG I made three raids on coastal positions between Nieuport and Oost Dunkirk dropping 6,000 kg/13,200 lb of bombs. Only one Allied aircraft – a Sopwith – intercepted the bombers but was shot to pieces by fighters of Jasta 17 long before he posed any threat. This was probably Sopwith Camel N6361 of 4 Naval Squadron, which was shot down between Pervijze and Ramskapelle at 7.50 pm. The plane crashed south of Nieuport, killing Second Lieutenant Busby.

Five Jastas – 7, 8, 17, 20 and the Marinejagdstaffel – supported aerial operations throughout that day and the next. They too flew to a strict timetable: every fighter squadron spent an hour and a half in the air, then the same period on stand-by at its base.

Operation Beach-Party was a resounding German victory. Without great loss they captured the British stronghold – all according to schedule. The aerial operation was also a great success, proving that it was possible to communicate by radio with six planes by using six different wavelengths. In addition the offensive role played by the two-seater squadrons had proved invaluable in supporting the attacking infantry during the battle – flying just above the advancing infantry, they spread panic among the

Albatros DVs of a Marinejagdstaffel take off from Aartrijke in late summer. The plane of Leutnant zur See Sachsenberg, Commanding Officer of I Marinefeldjagdstaffel, is decorated with a black and white chequered band around the fuselage (Collection O'Connor, UK).

enemy, throwing them into disarray. Enemy opposition in the air had been very limited, which explains why it was not necessary to send in the might of JG I.

Operation Beach-Party, carried out in adverse weather conditions, but with total air superiority, and making highly effective use of infantry support aircraft, became the blueprint for future German aerial operations.

The Third Battle of Ypres

31 July 1917
At 3.50 on the morning of the last day of July, the Allies launched a major offensive in Flanders. Twelve divisions of the British Fifth Army went over the top, supported by 3,535 guns and 800 aircraft. Germany had dug in 18 divisions with 1,162 guns and 640 aircraft ready for battle. A nasty surprise awaited the attacking troops – not only were they hampered by barbed wire and shell-holes filled with water, but the incessant rain of the previous days had turned the field into a sea of mud. German reconnaissance crews described the terrain:

A wooden hangar and a tent, damaged by Allied bombardment at Schusta 7's base at Moorsele, 7 July 1917 (collection Haerynck Belgium).

> *The terrain on both sides of the front line has become a tangle of craters and a veritable swamp. This makes any rapid advance by the troops impossible.*

The British now deployed their new weapon – the tank – but it proved ineffective in such muddy terrain, and they all sank into the swamp and were destroyed. The British also sent wave after wave of aircraft to attack the German positions in support of their advance – but at noon there was another downpour, making effective aerial support much more difficult. They had to fly below 60 m/200 ft and this led to heavy losses among the ground-attack planes.

Sopwith Camels loaded with four 9-kg/20-lb Cooper bombs slung under the fuselage flew in support of the Allied advance, and also made forays deep into German territory to attack airfields and rail transport.

At the start of the Third Battle of Ypres, German Group Ypres was the strongest in the air force with 17 units: Grufl 15, Jastas 3, 8, 26 and 27, FAs 7, 19, 45, (A) 202, 213, 221, 256 and Schustas 4, 11, 13, 23 and 30.

Group Wijtschate was the next strongest with 15 units: Grufl 7, Jastas 18, 24, 31 and 36, FAs 6, 8, 26, 33, (A) 250 and 294 and Schustas 7, 17, 24 and 25.

Next came Group Dixmude with Jastas 7, 29, 33 and 35, Flieger-Abteilungen 40, 48, (A) 231, 233 and 238 and Schustas 4, 16, 26 and 28.

Group North had 11 units: I and II MFFA, Marinefeldjasta, Kest 8, Jastas 20

and 28, FAs 231, 269, 293 and Kampfstaffel 1 and 23.

In the south, the small Group Lille consisted of Grufl 14, Jasta 17 and FAs 204, 227, 258 and 266 and Schustas 19 and 21.

The *Armeeoberkommando* (High Command) or AOK of the Fourth Army had its own units: JG 1 (comprising Jastas 4, 6, 10 and 11) and Jasta 2, FA 3 with FA (A) 224, Schustas 10 and 12 and KGs 1 and 4 (each with 36 bombers) and *Reichenbildzug* (Mosaic section) or RBZ 2. This latter was a specialised photo reconnaissance unit which three Reichenbildner aircraft equipped with special cameras which produced a series of successive exposures on a strip of film instead of single exposures on the usual glass plates.

The Dixmude, Ypres and Wijtschate groups were in the heat of the battle, taking great risks to carry out their dangerous duties in the face of intense anti-aircraft fire and fierce opposition from enemy fighters. As the command of the Group Dixmude had no clear picture of the situation at the front, an infantry flyer of FA 48 made a contact patrol. Flying perilously through a hail of artillery shells, the crew were able to determine how far the Allies had advanced their most forward lines by the colour of the infantry uniforms – but to do this they had to fly at 60 m/200 ft or less, which made them an easy target. First the observer was shot and when the engine also took a hit the pilot made a forced landing in his own lines. However, he had delivered the required information, and observer Buchner was decorated for his bravery.

Aircraft of Group Wijtschate, FA (A) 221 based at Bisseghem flew in support of the 6th Bavarian Reserve Division. Its war diary recorded:

Five infantry flights, three bombing flights and one reconnaissance. Due to bad weather, DFW CV 836/17 lost its

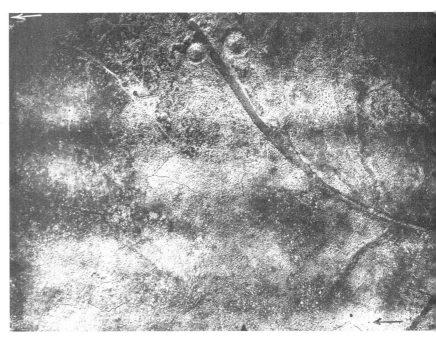

way and made an emergency landing near Torhout.

Many flying units earned special recognition from the High Command:

In the name of the whole division, I express the greatest respect to Flieger-Abteilung 33 and Schusta 7. Especially on Grosskampftag [the major day of combat] on 31 July, these units supported our infantry and artillery with exceptional courage. Their dangerous close support flights were an example to our troops and provided our High Command with vital information. Thanks to them, our guns could home in on the enemy batteries. Planes of the Schusta also took active part in the battle and played a large part in our successes. The men of Flieger-Abteilung 33 will always be etched on our memory.

JG I was only informed by phone at 11 am of the British breakthrough, but immediately sorties of two or four planes took off for the front and intervened in the dogfights between the German Jastas, British squadrons and French escadrilles.

The battlefield on 20 August 1917, with the trenches visible in the midst of the destroyed landscape. The black ribbon is the Menin-Ypres railway, and at the top are the two huge craters at Hill 60, the result of the mine detonations on 7 June (own collection).

Pilot	Jasta	Allied aircraft	Time	Location
Leutnant Hübner	4	Bristol	12.50 am	South of Zillebeke
Leutnant Meyer	11	RE	1.00 pm	West of Deimlingseck
Leutnant von Schönebeck	11	RE	1.10 pm	Above Frezenberg
Oberleutnant Dostler	6	Nieuport	2.05 pm	West of Bellewaerde Lake
Vizefeldwebel Wüsthoff	4	FE		Above Verbrandemolen
Unteroffizier Reinhold	24	F Sopwith triplane		Above Bailleul
Leutnant Gottsch	8	FE-biplane		Moorslede

In the first fortnight of the battle, the British lost 30 planes, and shot down only six.

Kurt Wüsthoff of Jasta 4 with his mechanics in front of an Albatros fighter at Marckebeke. He scored some 28 victories in the Flanders campaign, 14 of these in September 1917, and was awarded the Pour le Mérite on 22 November 1917 (Collection Maertens).

August 1917

Storms and heavy rain hampered aerial activity making flying impossible on 1, 2, 3 and 6 August, then low clouds and showers made it very difficult for the pilots to join the battle until early September. Despite the adverse conditions, the British managed to overrun the German defences near Gheluvelt on 10 August and near Langemark, further north, on 16 August.

It was sunny on 9 August – one of very few sunny days that month. The log books of Group Dixmude for that day give a picture of events:

The Group had 82 combat-ready planes and carried out 84 front-line flights.

They helped give accurate range to the artillery under difficult circumstances – an aircraft of Flieger-Abteilung (A) 231 could not give range to our artillery because grenades were ineffective in the swampy ground. A crew of Flieger-Abteilung (A) 256 had to stop directing artillery fire on the bridge across the Steenbeek because too many other batteries were firing on the same bridge. The aircraft also attacked the trenches from low altitude, flying at a dangerous 40 m/130 ft.

Flieger-Abteilung (A) 233 fired 150 rounds on positions near Oostkerke, Flieger-Abteilung (A) 231 targeted 30 rounds on trenches south of Dixmude, Flieger-Abteilung 48B fifty rounds on the lines near Noordschote. Five planes of Schusta 28 fired 1,260 rounds at trenches in front of the 19th Landwehr Division and Schusta 4 fired 290 shots on trenches to the west of Wijdendrift. Flieger-Abteilung 48B threw 200 kg/ 440 lb of bombs on Oostvleteren railway-station, Flieger-Abteilung 40 dropped 75 kg/165 lb on batteries south-east of Ypres, Schusta 26, 150 kg/330 of bombs on Oostvleteren and St-Jacobskapelle and Schusta 4, 162.5 kg/340 lb on Elverdinge Station. In addition, a large squadron formed by aircraft of Flieger-Abteilung 48B and Schustas 4 and 26 under the command of Oberleutnant Herrmann, dropped 785.5 kg/1,953 lb bombs on Oostvleteren Station.

Several units were involved in aerial combat. Leutnant Billick of Jasta 7 shot down a Spad, the Schusta 16 crew of Gefreiter Borchert and Flieger Kraatz forced down a Ponnier. Everywhere we were facing a superior enemy.

We lost three aircraft – crew of Flieger-Abteilung (A) 231 crashed from a height of 150 m/500 ft for an unknown reason, a plane of Flieger-Abteilung 40 crashed during take-off and a plane of Schusta 16 made a forced landing inside our lines.

Group Dixmude command was very satisfied with the performance of its aircrews:

Since 31 July, and in spite of adverse weather conditions and enemy air superiority, the airmen of the Group achieved excellent results. Their detailed and accurate information was invaluable for the commanders and their courageous sorties supported our ground troops superbly. They also recorded 22 victories during the first two weeks of August: two balloons and 20 aircraft.

Between 12 and 18 August, Schusta 11 downed three enemy planes. The Commander of the Group Ypres gave the three crews a 150-Mark bonus in appreciation of their achievements.

Suspended just behind the enemy front line, some 20 observation balloons monitored German movements. These aerials spies were the targets of many German attacks and a pilot of Jasta 26 described one such sortie:

12 August 1917. Today I received orders to attack a balloon. From 5.20 till 5.40 pm our artillery would fire on the nearby anti-aircraft guns that were protecting the balloon. Two colleagues would escort me. I had to hurry – there was a briefing with my two companions, loading suitable ammunition and then testing my engine. On the stroke of five we took off and sneaked across the front at 3,000 m/10,000 ft. The weather was fine but the anti-aircraft guns were not very accurate. Of the three balloons that I saw above the horizon, I choose the shiniest one. But then all at once three enemy single-seaters appeared right in front of us – the balloon's guardian angels. I attacked the plane closest to me, and he dived to avoid me, opening up the way for me. The two observers abandoned the balloon by parachute and I flew straight on towards the giant and fired 50 rounds. I almost collided with the balloon and expected that it would catch fire – but nothing happened. I attacked a second time – and then it burst into flames in more than 20 places.

I headed for home pursued by four enemy fighters, which delivered an absolute storm of fire. I flew on at 300 m/1,000 ft, and it was with a howl of joy that I regained my own lines and saw five Albatros flying above me. German planes! I was safe!'

A German Drachen AE observation balloon near Dadizele, between Roulers and Menin, over a typical Flemish farm, winter 1917. The German AE (Achthundert English) or English 800 was a copy of the French Caquot balloon – the 800 refers to its gas capacity of 800 cubic metres (Collection Raven).

On 21 August the Jastas recorded one of their best scores of the Third Battle of Ypres, downing 15 enemy aircraft. The chart gives a record of the day's victories:

Time	Pilot	Unit	Aircraft	Location
8.10	Leutnant Bolle	Jasta 28	Martinsyde	Seclin (France)
8.17	Oberleutnant Berthold	Jasta 18	Martinsyde	Dixmude
9.00	Offizier Stellvertreter Müller	Jasta 28	Martinsyde	La Bassée (France)
9.50	Leutnant Hess	Jasta 28	Sopwith two-seater	Ypres
10.25	Leutnant Hess	Jasta 28	RE	Verloren Hoek
10.30	Leutnant von Lieres	Jasta 29	RE	Langemark
12.08	Oberleutnant Dostler	Jasta 6	Biplane	Zonnebeke
19.30	Offizier Stellvertreter Müller	Js. 28	De Havilland	Ledegem
19.30	Unknown		Triplane	Beselare
19.30	Leutnant Wells	Jasta 28	Single-seater	Ypres
19.35	Leutnant Hanko	Jasta 28	De Havilland	Zonnebeke
20.14	Leutnant Loerzer	Jasta 26	Nieuport	Westrozebeke
20.15	Unknown		Sopwith	Passchendaele
20.15	Feldwebel Franke	Jasta 8	Sopwith	Passchendaele
20.20	Leutnant Danhuber	Jasta 26	Nieuport	Poelkapelle

That day Jasta 28 top-scored with seven victories and, with 32 overall, it remained the most successful squadron during August and September.

The Jastas were especially active during the morning and evening – and for good reason. It was important for headquarters to be apprised of the situation at the front at these particular times of day, so a lot of reconnaissance aircraft were in operation.

The Jastas confronted increasingly large groups of enemy aircraft – Leutnant Strähle of Jasta 18 recorded in his war diary:

17 August 1917. Leutnant Veltjens and I attacked five Spads below us and about

Fokker Dr I at Heule airfield, winter 1917-1918 (Collection Nielebock Germany).

The LFG Roland D III was an inferior fighter aircraft compared with other contemporary fighters available to the German Army, especially those produced by Albatros. This aircraft was therefore only produced in small quantities, but Jasta 35 was still using it in September 1917 (own collection).

12 enemy single-seaters dived down on me from above.

Sometimes the enemy numbers were just too big. On 25 August Leutnant der Reserve Jacobs (Jasta 7) found himself outnumbered:

It was very bad weather. I took off with my group at 3.10 pm. At the front near Ypres there was a great deal of activity by infantry-support aircraft. Because we were heavily outnumbered and because the turbulent weather made shooting impossible, we flew back.

Dogfights could often last for up to an hour, with aircraft flying at altitudes from 300 - 6,000 m/1,000 - 18,000 ft and individual groups entering into the fight as others broke off.

The increase in the number of dogfights prompted headquarters to investigate new tactics to achieve better results over the battlefields, and from the end of August the German High Command scrambled its Jastas

Group	Jagdgruppe	Jastas	Airfield	Commander
Wijtschate	Jg 7	18, 24, 31, 36	Cuerne Harlebeke-Bavikhove	Oberleutnant Berthold
Ypres	Jg 15	3, 8, 26, 27	Iseghem Rumbeke	Hauptmann von Bentheim
Dixmude	Jg 11	7, 29, 33, 35	Aartrijke	Oberleutnant Schmidt
North	Jg Nord	2, 28, 29 Kest 8	Jabbeke	Hauptmann Hartmann

in larger formations. This tactic produced better co-ordination between the Jastas as demonstrated by this war diary extract:

24 August. Operation to retake the Herentageposten at Polygon near Gheluvelt. Infantry and artillery planes, Jasta 24 at 2,000 m/6,500 ft. Jasta 18 between 3,500 and 4,200 m/11,500 and 1,3000 ft. No enemy opposition. The assault was a complete success.

The Fourth Army's fighter squadrons had notched up 116 victories by the end of August, with Group North's Jasta 28 the most successful with 22 wins. Jasta 11 of (JG I) was also very effective with 14 victories and Jasta 3 of Group Ypres with 11. On the other hand the Jastas lost five pilots.

September 1917

Despite tough resistance from the German Jastas and the loss of 120 aircraft, the Allies reclaimed aerial superiority during that month. Leutnant der Reserve Jacobs of Jasta 7 recorded in his diary:

3 September. It was a great day for us as we shot down five enemy aircraft.

I took off with two formations (Leutnant Meyer, Kunst, Thun, Degelow and myself, and Leutnant Billik, Vizefeldwebel Horst, Techow, Leutnant Kunz) around 7.40 am. We'd been patrolling along the front for some time when there was shooting near our airfield. I quickly spotted an enemy formation, so we went after them in high spirits. I saw one of our aircraft being hotly pursued, so I went to his assistance but I was too late and the Albatros exploded. Then I got a Sopwith single-seater perfectly in my sights, but was attacked by a Spad. I wanted to make a steep turn but lost control and somersaulted – and down I went, unable to stop myself. When I regained control I flew home. Soon my men returned and put in their report: Leutnant Meyer shot a Sopwith down in flames over Dixmude, Leutnant Billik forced a Sopwith down inside our lines, Leutnant Degelow forced a Sopwith to land in enemy lines and Leutnant Thun shot down a Spad. It was a splendid day for our still quite inexperienced squadron.

11 September. At 6.15 pm Leutnant der Reserve Güttler (Jasta 24) jumped a Sopwith triplane north-west of Bellewaerde. The plane tumbled and fell and Güttler attacked a second time. After this attack it dived vertically, but he couldn't see the impact due to the

ground mist and darkness. This crash was witnessed by Leutnant Friedrich Nielebock, an observer with FA (A) 250.

During the first week of September the German air force lost 11 planes in Flanders and this got no better over the next weeks, with a number of aces among the casualties. On 3 September, Otto Hartmann, commander of Jasta 28, was shot down and killed north of Dixmude by a crew of 48 Squadron RFC, and even JG I suffered bad losses. Karl Bodenschatz recorded in his war diary:

15 September. Killed: Oberleutnant Wolff (commander of Jasta 11) at 5.30 pm, north of Wervicq in an aerial combat. His plane, a Fokker triplane FI 102, was destroyed.

23 September. Killed: Leutnant Voss (Jasta 10). He took off at 6.05 pm with his squadron and probably crashed in enemy lines while engaged in aerial combat. Plane: Fokker triplane.

25 September. Killed: Oberleutnant Weigand (Jasta 10), shot down in flames at 5.40 pm above Houthulst Forest during aerial combat.

On 11 September German fighters inflicted a severe blow on the Allied air forces by shooting down the French hero Georges Guynemer above Poelkapelle. The flying ace was at the height of his popularity and to the French troops and people alike he was as good as a god.

In mid-July Guynemer's unit was sent to St-Pol airfield near Dunkirk. His group comprised the very best of the French escadrilles: Spa 3, Spa 26, Spa 73 and Spa 103. Guynemer of Spa 3 had already claimed 48 victories and he scored five more confirmed over Flanders – four reconnaissance aircraft and one fighter.

Plane	Location	Date	Number of victory
Albatros	Between Roulers and Langemark	27 July	49
DFW	Westrozebeke	28 July	50
Albatros two-seater	Vladsloo	17 August	51
DFW	Dixmude	17 August	52
Two-seater	Staden	18 August	not confirmed
DFW	Poperinghe	20 August	53

How he came to be killed remains a mystery. There is almost no evidence and no-one has ever found the exact location where he crashed. On the morning of Tuesday 11 September he took off at 8.25 together with Sous-lieutenant (second lieutenant) Bozon-Verduraz. He began a patrol deep inside German-held territory above the front line near Poelkapelle, while Bozon-Verturaz patrolled above the lines, waiting for his famous colleague… but Guynemer never came back. It was most probably Leutnant Wisseman of Jasta 3 who shot him down, and as his plane crashed in the German lines it would have been found by a German patrol.

A German infantryman reported:

I was having a wash just outside one of our bunkers when I heard, high in the sky, the sound of aerial combat, however, I could not see the duelling planes because there was a thick layer of cloud. All of a sudden there was a loud screeching sound. I expected it was a British gas attack and jumped into the bunker, but instead of an explosion I heard the sound of breaking wood. From experience I knew that a plane had come down.

I went to search for the plane with some of my men and we found the totally wrecked aircraft some 200 m/220 yd from our shelter. We couldn't see the pilot either in the wreck or in the surrounding area. We started to strip the engine, which was stuck some 0.5 m/2 ft in the mud, and there at the bottom we found the dead body of the pilot. In his breast pocket we found the name of the victim – Lieutenant Guynemer. This name was not totally unknown to us because we'd all heard about the famous French pilot. We thought maybe we had

The memorial dedicated to Lieutenant Georges Guynemer at Poelkapelle. On top is the stork emblem, the insignia of Groupe de Combat 12 (own collection).

found a relative of the famous ace but a couple of days later our HQ confirmed that it was after all the famous pilot.

Over the next days the French aircraft was destroyed by enemy fire and sank without trace into the swampy ground.

The German air force was still outnumbered in the sky above Flanders, but in spite of their inferior numbers they managed to inflict some serious damage on their Allied counterparts, as this report from German HQ attests:

In spite of bad weather our flying units made their presence felt. Every day our contact patrol crews succeeded in monitoring the development of the front line. The artillery support crews achieved good results in directing fire, even on distant targets.

The few days of fair weather were quite enough for our reconnaissance crews to register and record almost everything happening in enemy territory, and they also carried out an important photographic survey of the area.

On moonlit nights our crews made significant bombing raids, whose success was proven by huge fires and explosions. Kampfgeschwader 1 and 4 dropped 30,000 kg/6,600 lb of bombs on St-Omer, Dunkirk, Boulogne, Dover, Calais and the ammunition dumps of Bailleul, Audruicq and Hazebrouck.

Oberleutnant Krausser and Unteroffizier Schönemann of Schusta 23 deserve a special mention. On the nights of 2/3 and 4/5 September they made four bombing sorties and dropped 1,000 kg/2,200 lb of bombs.

Several times during recent weeks our fighter squadrons could have toppled the Allies' aerial superiority.

It wasn't until 20 September that the British ground troops attacked again, advancing along the Menin road. The war

Six Rumpler CIVs of FA 8 on Bavikhove airfield (6 September 1917). Notice the large spinner and the semi-circular radiator.

diary of Leutnant der Reserve Jacobs of Jasta 7 recorded:

Today there was very bad weather at the front. All last night we heard continuous gunfire and the windows and doors in the castle were rattling.

On 26 September the British stormed Polygon Wood and the fighting was fierce. Preceded by heavy shelling, British forces penetrated the German trenches and captured their bunkers, however, the German defenders clung to every position and prevented a decisive Allied breakthrough.

The role of aircraft in these ground attacks became increasingly important. During the heavy fighting of 19 and 20 September Schusta 23 carried out a daring low level attack against British troops

losing or damaging five of its six planes, as described in the CO's account:

As the summer of 1917 drew to a close, the British prepared to renew the Flanders offensive by pushing forward along the Menin Road toward Gheluvelt plateau on 20 September. It had been dry for much of the month, but on the eve of this attack the rains returned, drenching the skies and battlefield. At Ingelmunster, 18 km/11 miles behind the front lines, the pilots, observers and mechanics of Schusta 23 and Flieger-Abteilung 19 could clearly hear the artillery fire to the west. Windowpanes rattled and the walls vibrated in their quarters. Everyone waited anxiously for the order to fly, but the weather made that impossible. However, within a few hours, Schusta 23

Armoured Junkers JI of Flieger-Abteilung (A) 250 returning after a sortie (Collection Nielebock).

An LVG CV of
Flieger-Abteilung
(A) 250 at Heule,
late 1917. The
box fitted between
the interplane
struts indicates
altitude and
time. The small
propeller fitted
to the strut is a
Morell airspeed
indicator of the
anemometer
type, which
was standard
equipment on
German aircraft
(Collection
Nielebock).

would have one of their busiest and gruelling days ever.

During the night of 19 September the roaring thunder rages furiously outside. There's a crash and a windowpane in my room shatters on the floor. I can no longer remain in bed. It is 4 am and pitch black, and the rain is being whipped up by the strong wind. This damned Flanders weather! But I have an indefinable feeling… 'Today we'll be going.'

Rrrrrr! Rrrr! Rrrrrr! A crack of 'thunder' startles me. Yes, gradually even the strongest nerves go to the devil… but it is only the telephone. 'What's up?' 'The duty officer of Flieger-Abteilung 19 here. At dawn we must send a crew over the 121st Division's sector and I request an escort for them. In addition, the division is asking for several ground attack planes to be made ready for today. They're expecting an assault.'

'Jawohl! Everything will be done. It is now 4.30 and in another hour it will be light. At 5.45 the escort aircraft will be ready to start outside its hangar. Good morning!'

I quickly look at the duty roster to see who's up first today. Ah ha, here it is – escort flight on 20 September: aircraft No 6, crew: Vizefeldwebel Möhlenbeck and Unteroffizier Bitzer. For infantry attack: aircraft Nos 3, 4 and 5.

In reserve: No. 2. Under repair: No 1. Getting back on the telephone I call the airfield office to alert the squadron and have the machines and crews made ready. They are to gather in the first hangar. Today we will have something to do!

Shortly after that the sound of the distant artillery fire increases in intensity. It has been like this since 31 July with only a few short breaks. Nevertheless, through mud and blood the English keep coming on, slowly but stubbornly – but there is always the German infantry in front of them.

At 5.15 I reach the airfield to find everyone already there. The engines of five machines are running, their noise in the darkness temporarily masking the rumble of the gunfire. The mechanics are still zealously at their work, the chief grumbling and swearing. The armourer and his assistants bring up the machine-guns and belts of ammunition, and test one by firing a short burst into the rainy sky. In Hangar No 1 the crews are waiting – my 11 'brothers' – even though I have been with them only three months.

Möhlenbeck and Bitzer report themselves ready to fly. They have not been in the squadron for very long, but I am glad to have them. Both are quiet, brave men who always do their duty without many words. One is a Prussian while the other a Bavarian from Swabia; nevertheless, they have become true comrades.

Both receive their orders: to fly over to Flieger-Abteilung 19's airfield and report as escort for that squadron's infantry-support flight. Bitzer waves as he and Möhlenbeck disappear around the corner of the hangar and run to their machine. I will never see them again.

The other four planes are ready. We wait. At 7 am we receive a message from the division: 'Heavy English attack in progress. Our most forward troops in the Wilhelmstellung have been pushed back but the position is still in our hands.' We carry on waiting. More uncertainty! Then, at 8.20 am, the telephone rattles again.

'The 121st Infantry Division here. The division needs your support immediately for a counter-attack from the Wilhelmstellung. The infantry is ready to go.'

'All right! In 20 minutes at the last three aircraft will be over your positions.'

The waiting crews spring to life. We are already muffled up in our leather flying clothes. I quickly give the pilots and their gunners a briefing of the situation and the order: 'Aircraft 3 and 5 fly behind me. I will lead in No 4. At my flare signal, begin the attack with machine guns and hand-grenades, targeting any Englishmen you see. Hals und Beinbruch!'*

[* Literally, 'Neck and leg break' – as in 'Break a leg' for luck.]

Flying helmets and goggles are on. The first aircraft to take off, No 5, roars over the airfield. My machine, flown by Vizefeldwebel Weidner, starts last, though only a minute after the other two. The rain is still coming down in sheets, lashing our faces, and every five seconds I have to wipe my goggles in order to see. The clouds hang just 100 m/360 ft above the ground, and because of them we can't climb any higher.

We fly over the Iseghem-Roulers railway line at Roulers and from there we follow along the line toward Ypres. If we don't we may not be able to find the division's sector in the mud. Above our artillery positions the plane is buffeted up and down and from side to side. We note the 'acceptable' proximity of our German shells hurtling past us through the rain on their way towards the English. We are getting closer to the front.

Moorslede comes into view – we are over it already. Below, enemy shells are crashing down. Thick 'trees' of smoke grow from the earth following the shuddering red flashes of the explosions. A German ammunition dump is thrown up into the air. To us it looks like a harmless fireworks display. Further, further! Now we can see people lying here and there in the water – and slime-filled craters – they are German infantrymen. My God, how they must be suffering! They stare up at us with white faces. Several wave their handkerchiefs and caps. I wave back. Yes, you poor, brave fellows. We're here to help you.

We fly further forward, on into the barren battle zone. Below is a picture of hell with the blasts and smoke of exploding shells. Suddenly, darkness surrounds us – a low-hanging cloud obscures the view below us. We must go through it. When we do and can see again, something passes close by. It is an enemy machine bearing cockades and a pennant. He seems startled by our sudden appearance from the cloud and immediately tries to clear out. [Low flying aircraft were distinguished by two long streamers on the wing struts to avoid friendly fire.]

'Get him, Weidner!' I yell to my pilot. He takes quick aim and fires forward through the propeller with his machine-gun. Unfortunately, the Tommy has a faster machine and begins to put distance between us. Flying at full throttle, we press on from behind, my eyes fixed firmly on the enemy. He flies lower – our altimeter shows 50m /180 ft. To the left of us, forward and somewhat higher, is machine No 3 of our squadron. I

The briefing of
a new observer
before take-off
in a DFW CV
(Collection
Haerynck
Belgium).

cannot find No 5. Suddenly, a noise
like hundreds of caps detonating hits
me in the ear. Almost simultaneously
I see No 3 speed past us in a steep left
turn and head for home. What could
be wrong? Has the crew lost its pluck?
They disappear. Below us lay the ruins of
Frezenberg that we have come to know
well since the beginning of the battle in
Flanders.

The sharp, staccato noise grows
stronger. It is not very reassuring to us
for we know the sound is machine-gun
and rifle fire. We've already heard several
suspicious 'thumps' in the fuselage. I
estimate we are now about 5 km/3 miles
behind the front – and only 50 m/150
ft high. I keep looking for something to
attack below. There! A battery out in the
open! They open fire on us. We fly over,
first throwing four hand-grenades and
then letting off a hail of machine-gun fire

at them. They run, crawl and jump into
shell holes, but there is little protective
cover.

The battery is silent, though the
continuing gunfire makes me somewhat
uncomfortable. Weidner banks, but it
does not take long until we hear more
'thumps' in our machine. We both know
from experience what this means and
now we're getting more than our fair
share. But where? We listen anxiously
to the engine, but it hums quietly. That
is good, for if we were to make a forced
landing here we would surely end up as
prisoners, or be killed.

There is no time to search further
for holes in the machine. I return to
my machine-gun and fire over the side
– 100, 150, 250 rounds. The belt is
empty. Weidner has 1,000 rounds for his
machine-gun. He continuously dips the
plane's nose forward and fires ahead – he

has plenty of targets. The shell-holes are packed thick with Tommies.

Finally we are over Moorslede again – our rendezvous point. However, my other two aircraft are nowhere to be seen. As we circle I load a new ammunition belt into the gun. Tension and excitement shoot through my entire body, and although I don't know why my feet begin shivering. By chance I look down ... and see a perfect mess! Fuel is pouring through the airplane! So that's the result of the 'thumps'. I slap Weidner on the shoulder and yell to him that we've taken a hit in the petrol tank. He nods. He always nods, never getting excited. Shouting, I ask him, 'Can we make another run?' Glancing at the petrol-gauge, he nods again. 'All right, let's go!' A fine spray of vaporised fuel several metres long trails behind us.

Both of my escorts have disappeared without a trace and we fly on alone. We are soon over English territory again. Everywhere we fire, the enemy runs for it, though we avoid shooting at horses. If only we had just 20 or 30 planes with us! Such an attack would hit the English hard, but alone we can do only so much damage. I have just finished another belt of ammunition and silently compliment my efficient armourer. I have not had a single jam. On our return flight I see infantrymen for the first time in our forwardmost line. They are difficult to find. There lie two, there three and there a group of four or five men with a machine-gun. It is men such as these who are holding up the great English attack. But they are no longer occupying the Wilhelmstellung and I can see nothing resembling a counter-attack. The poor fellows below signal to me, waving with anything they have – helmets, rifles, caps and handkerchiefs. Apparently our presence has given them something to cheer about, and that fills

me with great pride. I wave back as long as I can see them, but soon we are back over Moorslede. At least, that is what it is called on the map. In reality it is only a heap of stones and brick.

The old game repeats itself: I load another belt of ammunition, search in vain for my two other aircraft and ask Weidner if we can go back still one more time. Again he nods. The spray of fuel remains our only 'escort', floating behind us. For a third time we dive, firing at the enemy. Thank God the accursed rain has let up somewhat and I am now able to see better. At 50 m/150 ft height we fly back and forth until Weidner and I have both fired off all our ammunition. It's time to return to our airfield since it would be foolish to further risk our beautifully shot-up machine with a forced landing in the cratered fields below. We still have 25 litres of fuel, but that is quickly gushing out through the hole in the tank. With a strong backwind we reach the field in 10 minutes and land smoothly. I am met by the crew of No 5 and learn that they had been quite near us through most of the flight. Only when we began our third attack had they been forced to return due to a shortage of ammunition – and their crate showed a good number of holes.

The crews of No 2 (which until now was held in reserve) and No 5 immediately receive orders to attack the English lying in and in front of the Wilhelmstellung. Unfortunately, Weidner and I in No 4 can not return with them. Nos 3 and 6 still are missing. They cannot be in the air for it has already been considerably longer than three hours since they had taken off.

Shortly after 9 am, Nos 2 and 5 start and come back safely about an hour later, although they are badly shot up after making several attacks. Both will have to be dismantled and repaired. My squadron is 'finished'. There is nothing remaining for me to do except to see that the three aircraft are patched up as quickly as possible, to have reports made, and to begin a search for my two missing crews. We are all very worried.

Finally, at 3 pm, a telephone message comes in from Unteroffizier Schwarz, the gunner of plane No 3. He says that his pilot, Unteroffizier Jokisch, was hit by a bullet in the middle of the chest during their first attack at a height of 50 m/150 ft. At the same time their engine and petrol tank were struck. In spite of this, Jokisch brought the plane down without mishap in a cratered meadow near Dadizele – a laudable performance considering the weather was very stormy and unfavourable for a forced landing. Immediately after coming down he was taken to a field hospital in Winkel St Elooi. The plane was still near Dadizele. It had more than 30 holes in it, including one in the petrol tank and three in the engine.

Unfortunately the search for Möhlenbeck and Bitzer goes on without success. The first news we receive comes on the evening of 24 September: aircraft No 6 is found totally destroyed in a cratered field near Westrozebeke, both occupants lying dead next to the wreckage. After much difficulty their bodies are recovered on 28 September and sent back to Germany. The death of Unteroffizier Bitzer is especially tragic, for shortly after he had taken off with Möhlenbeck that day, his Iron Cross arrived at the airfield office. He will never wear it.

On 26 September the British stormed Polygon Wood, but although the Germans were overrun, they ceded only a small amount of territory to the British.

These Allied attacks were not a total surprise to the German command, as thanks to reconnaissance reports from FA 3 and *Reichenbildzug* (Mosaic section) or RBZ 2 they were largely able to predict the Allied initiatives. These two units were mainly used for strategic long-distance reconnaissance and photographic missions far behind the enemy lines. It was not easy for them to enter the well-guarded Allied air space but they managed it by flying via the North Sea.

From 6 June 1917 onwards, RBZ 2 was operational in Flanders, flying from Bavikhove, and working in close co-operation with FA 3 to provide detailed aerial reconnaissance with the mosaic-style multi-image photography. A report of 27 September 1917 shows the type of work carried out by RBZ 2:

On 24 and 25 September our three crews captured excellent images of the region directly behind the front line.

1. There is dense traffic in front of Group Ypres. Only a few vehicles are parked. This confirms the offensive that started yesterday in this sector.

2. Special attention was paid to the armoured trains. The railway network has been extended and we found several armoured trains directed at our positions: 28 in front of Group Dixmude, six in front of Group Nord and 16 in front of Group Ypres. These high concentrations of railway-mounted guns probably indicate a new offensive in the near future.

3. The sheer numbers of troops and the dense traffic in the sector in front of Group Ypres suggest that the offensive will continue for some time.

The Jastas of Group Wijtschate (numbers 18, 24 and 36) were present en masse over the hazardous British lines at Polygon Wood and shot down 27 enemy planes between 20 and 30 September, during which time Oberleutnant Rudolf Berthold,

CO of Jasta 36, was the highest scoring pilot with seven victories. The four elite Jastas of JG I were ordered to reinforce Group Wijtschate, as shown in their war diary for 20 September.

Leutnant Adam (Jasta 6) downed a Sopwith at 6.40 am west of Bellewaerde above enemy territory as his seventeenth victory. Ten minutes later he downed another Sopwith over Beselare. At the same time, also over Beselare, Leutnant Stock (Jasta 6) shot down a triplane – his first victory. Leutnant Wüsthoff (Jasta 4) claimed his eighteenth victory – a Spad at 12.15 am over the hamlet of America. Oberleutnant Döring (Jasta 4) downed a Spad at 12.30 am, south of Ypres and above the enemy territory. It is his eighth victory. Vize-Feldwebel Bachmann (Jasta 6) shot down an observation balloon near Kemmel at 2.00 pm. Wüsthoff scored a second time at 2.30 pm, downing a Spad west of Langemark.

At 11.30 am Leutnant Löwenhardt (Jasta 10) was slightly wounded and made a forced landing near Roulers.

Leutnant Just (Jasta 11) took a hit to his petrol tank and made an emergency landing near Beselare.

The squadron made 101 sorties during the day. Our aircraft were outnumbered in a ratio of two to one.

This high concentration of German fighter units over the sector kept the British airmen at bay. Jasta 36 victoriously reported in its war diary:

Because of our victories, the enemy was not to be seen for the next few days!

October and November

During October the Allies kept up a series of offensives. British, Canadian, Australian and New Zealand troops launched attacks between Langemark in the north and Gheluvelt in the south (Battle of Broodseinde) on 4 October, then on 9 October (Battle of Poelkapelle), 12 October (First Battle of Passchendaele) and 26 October (Second Battle of Passchendaele). These advances were constantly hampered by bad weather, but by the end of the month the Canadians had reached the ruins of Passchendaele village.

In response Germany brought in reinforcements and on 10 October FA (A) 211 arrived at Torhout, and six days later FA 32 moved to Ondank near Winghene.

To optimise their defences, a new German Army Group was formed on 8 October – Group Staden, located between Group Dixmude and Group Ypres. From that point the Fourth Army's air support was organised as follows:

Group Lille
  a) Grufl 12
  b) One unit flying for Group HQ: FA (A) 258
  c) Three units flying for the divisions: FA (A) 227, 266 and 294 B with their Schustas 21 and 27 B
  d) Jasta17

The grave of one of the Red Baron's victims, Second Lieutenant James Edward Power-Clutterbuck of 53 Squadron RFC, who was downed above Le Bizet flying as an observer in a RE8. He is buried in the Strand Military Cemetery in Ploegsteert (own collection).

Group Wijtschate
a) Grufl 7
b) Two units flying for Group HQ: FA 8 and 13 (FA 13 had moved to the Fourth Army early in October)
c) Four units flying for the divisions: FA 6, 33, (A) 221 and 250 and their Schustas: 30B, 17, 24B and 7
d) One fighter group with Jastas 18, 24 and 36

Group Ypres
a) Grufl 15
b) Two units flying for Group HQ: FA 7 and FA (A) 202 with Schusta 18
c) Three units flying for the divisions: FA 26, 19 and FA (A) 238 with Schustas 28B, 23B and 9;
d) One fighter group with Jastas 26, 27 and Boelcke (Jasta 2)

Group Staden
a) Grufl 11
b) Two units flying for Group HQ: FA 40 and FA 32 with Schusta 12 seconded from Group Ypres
c) Three units flying for the divisions: FA 45B with Schusta 11, FA (A) 256 with Schusta 4 and FA (A) 213 with Schusta 13
d) One fighter group with Jastas 3, 33 and 37

Group Dixmude
a) Grufl 2
b) FA (A) 211 flying for Group HQ
c) Three units flying for the divisions: FA 48 B, FA (A) 233 and (A) 231 with two Schustas: 16 and 26 B
d) Jastas 7, 29 and 35B in one Jagdgruppe

Gruppe Nord or Marinekorps Flandern
a) Grufl Nord
b) I MFFA with Marine Schusta, II MFFA, FA (A) 269 and (A) 293. Schusta 29B flew for this last unit
c) Jagdgruppe Nord: Marine Jasta, Kest 8 and Jasta 28

The Jastas had to do their best under very difficult circumstances, as this report from German HQ attests:

9 October. 10.07 am Gefreiter Hegeler of Jasta 24 engaged two RE8s and one Nieuport in combat. The Nieuport was forced to land near Gheluwe, however, the victory was attributed to Jasta 11.

On 16 October Unteroffizier Reinhold (Jasta 24) was forced to land at Cuerne airfield (Jasta 36) after a combat. His landing gear, radiator and wing spar were all damaged by enemy fire.

20 October. At noon Leutnant Gerstenberg of Jasta 11 was hit in the lung and forced to make an emergency landing near Rollegem-Kapelle. At 1.10 pm Unteroffizier Hardel of Jasta 10 was hit in the leg during a dogfight. He broke his leg landing north of Courtrai.

26 October. Rain, clouds and strong wind. A formation of Jasta 18 flew above Roulers around 12 am. They opened fire on two enemy aircraft which were attacking our positions at about 1,200 m/4,000 ft. Klein and Schober attacked one, Strähle and Rahn the other. Unfortunately, Leutnant Schober was shot down by the Englishman. Strähle and Rahn fought a tough dogfight with the other for over a quarter of an hour, sometimes almost at ground level. They followed their quarry as far as Ichtegem where Strähle had to break off because his guns jammed.

During that month Jasta 36 claimed 26 victories without a single loss, but it was a hectic time for the FAs. FA (A) 221 flew above the southern sector of the Allied breakthrough, as reported in the unit's history:

Friday, 26 October. Heavy rain till 10.50 am. Flying above heavy artillery exchanges, two crews carried out three contact patrols near Gheluvelt.

The crew Johnke-Horn flew from 10.50 until 12.00 am and confirmed that Gheluvelt village was still in German

The valiant pilots of Jasta 36 before their take-off hut at Cuerne airfield (November). We can see Leutnant Lüdecke (1), Vizefeldwebel Patzer(2), Lt.d.R.Heinrich Bongartz (3), Lt Denkewitz (4), Lt.d.R. Hoyer (5), Staffel-Führer Walter von Bülow-Bothcamp with PLM (6), Lt Führmann (7), Lt.d.R. Harry von Bülow (8), Lt.d.R. Müller(9), Lt.d.R. von Haebler (10), Lt.d.R. Quandt (11) and Lt.d.R.Böhning (12) (own collection).

hands but they could not ascertain who occupied Château Polderhoek. They saw five of our companies moving forward across the château grounds and witnessed the massive explosion of an enemy ammunition dump south of the Menin-Ypres road. They were attacked several times by British fighters during their patrol.

Between 1.05 and 1.45 pm a contact patrol carried out by Classen-Zichäus: heavy shelling in the Gheluvelt-Daimlingseck area and from the Polderhoek grounds to Westhoek. Our own fire heavy from the west side of the grounds and 1 km behind the lines. They also made contact with our own troops. They spotted two white strips near Château Polderhoek, one signal near the road north of the 'H' of 'Haus Baden', and three white strips near 3188. They sprayed enemy positions on both sides of the Menin-Ypres road with machine-gun fire from low altitude.

Two hours later, from 3.45 until 4.30 pm, Johnke and Horn made a second contact patrol. They could define the front line thanks to the flare signals and the white strips spread out by the infantry. Enemy fire on the east side of the château grounds. Our fire was concentrated on Pattyn Farm. Due to the heavy rain they could not make out any concentrations of troops or enemy infiltration. Fired on trenches west of

Gheluvelt and Polderhoek with machine-gun from a height of 100 m/330 ft. No enemy planes, own aerial activity sparse.

A 50-minute bombing raid was carried out at 5.00 pm to disrupt enemy preparations for an assault on Château Polderhoek just outside Gheluvelt. Despite heavy rain, our six crews made a low-level attack on Pattyn Farm and the area south of it, firing 2,000 rounds and dropping 100 kg of bombs. They made the following reconnaissance report: enemy artillery less effective, the enemy kept firing green Very lights west of the Château Polderhoek grounds. A very active enemy battery at Y48 11/17. Our fire was accurate and concentrated between the Pattyn Farm and the western area of Gheluvelt. No signs of the enemy and a lot of our own aerial activity.

FA 33 was active in the same sector, as reported in the unit's war diary:

Saturday, 27 October. Contact patrol by the crew Ingenhofen-Manhold above the ruins of Gheluvelt at 8.00 am. The crew reported our troops in the south-west part of the village subject to heavy shelling. German mortars responded. Observer Manhold directed this fire using the wireless and dropping a message-bag. He also took 15 photographs.

FA (A) 211 flew above the northern edge of the enemy penetration. The unit's war diary recorded:

On 1 November our planes directed our artillery fire, destroying a very dangerous Allied battery.

The Third Battle of Ypres came to an end in early November and tension mounted in other areas of the Western Front. Germany reacted swiftly, sending some 40 flying units from Flanders to sectors under greater threat. Of the 22 Jastas in Flanders 14 left the Fourth Army. Group Dixmude lost all flying units but one – Flieger-Abteilung (A) 227. Oberleutnant Bechtle, a pilot with FA33, gave the reason for this re-organisation:

...during November we were hastily transferred to the tank battle at Cambrai...

Following the capture of the ruins of Passchendaele by the Canadians, both sides settled down to regroup. On 11 November the British command decided to halt the attack and by the 20 November the decision was taken to end the offensive. The Third Battle of Ypres was over and the Allied offensive had failed. They had hoped to clear the Germans from the Belgian coast but they only had progressed only 5 km/3 miles. The losses were very high with 240,000 British and 150,000 Germans killed.

The fighting around Ypres demonstrated that large-scale offensives could no longer be carried out without adequate aerial support, and from this point success on the ground was closely linked to the achievement of aerial superiority. The air force was now a vital factor in victory or defeat.

In the three and a half months of the Third Battle of Ypres the German air force notched up 570 victories; its reconnaissance units had made 2,560 artillery-ranging sorties and located 7,980 firing batteries. They also took 21,500 photographs and dropped some 750,000 kg/1,650,000 lb of bombs on artillery positions, bunkers, railway stations and harbours. On average some 8.5 planes were lost a day through crashes, enemy fire and accidents. Aircrew casualties amounted to nearly 37 per cent of the air force's total strength with 133 killed, 203 wounded or injured and 52 missing in action.

During November the Germans downed 80 enemy aircraft, but then December was a calm month. Low clouds, mist, snow and rain prevented flying for all but 18 days.

Despite the stagnation of the Allied advance in the Third Battle of Ypres, the Allies still enjoyed aerial superiority over Flanders at the close of 1917. There was a lot for the German command to do to reverse the situation in the coming year.

German Aircraft in 1917

During 1917, DFW, LVG, Rumpler, Albatros, Pfalz and Fokker aircraft were the main workhorses of the Jastas, FAs and Schustas.

Aircraft in service with Flieger-Abteilung (A) 221 were as follows:

January, February and March: Rumpler CI, Albatros CVII and CI

April, May and June: Albatros CVII, Rumpler CIV, AEG CIV and Albatros CV

July, August, September: Albatros CV, Albatros CX, DFW C V, Rumpler CIV, AEG JI

October, November and December: LVG CV, Rumpler CIV, Halberstadt CLII, AEG JI and Albatros JI

One of the most successful of the C-type planes, which were introduced during 1915, was the CI from the Rumpler Flugzeugwerke. By the end of 1916 there were still some 250 CIs in service and they were only superseded early in 1917.

Powered by a 160-hp Mercedes engine, the CI could carry a 100-kg/200-lb bomb-load. It was equipped with a fixed Spandau machine-gun forward and a Parabellum machine-gun for the observer.

The Rumpler factory replaced the CI during 1917 with the CIV, which had a 260-hp Mercedes engine. These new aircraft were mainly used in a strategic role on long-distance reconnaissance and photographic sorties, when its high-altitude performance was invaluable – there were few Allied fighters that could catch the CIV at high altitude.

Further development of the very successful CIV resulted in the CVII, which was fitted with a 240-hp Maybach engine that gave excellent performance at extreme altitude. A special photo-reconnaissance version was produced – the Rubild – which had

*The remains of a
Rumpler CIV, C8445,
which crashed on 11
November 1917 at
Poelkapelle. The machine-
gun has been removed
– the frontal radiator is
mounted at the leading
edge of the centre section
of the upper wing. The
radiator's semicircular
shape reduced the blind
spot area, which was a
problem with rectangular
radiators (Collection
Maertens).*

no forward armament fitted and was the highest-flying Rumpler with a ceiling of 7,800 m/24,000 ft. Even at 6,600 m/20,000 ft it could maintain a speed of 160 km/h/100 mph.

The CIV and CVII were of tough construction – on at least two occasions their crews survived crashing from a very high altitude. Leutnant Friedrich Hublitz of FA 32 crashed his CIV in October 1917, and pilot Walter Gabriel of FA (A) 250 who crashed near London in August 1917. A Rumpler CVII was also the first plane to carry out a night bombing raid on London on 7/8 May 1917.

The DFW (Deutsche Flugzeugwerke) CV was undoubtedly the best-liked plane among the FAs, fulfilling its role in reconnaissance, artillery co-operation and infantry contact patrols. In August 1917 some 1000 CVs were in service and 600 were still in front-line service right up to the end of hostilities. Very similar to the CV was the LVG (Luftverkehrsgesellschaft) CV – an excellent all-rounder for medium-range duties – which, with a wingspan of nearly 15 m/45 ft it was one of the largest of the German two-seaters. Equipped with the standard fixed and movable machine-guns and with a bomb-load of some 115 kg/230 lb it was used widely by the Schustas.

Other widely used two-seaters were the AEG CIV produced by the Allgemeine Elektrizitäts Gesellschaft and the Albatros Flugzeugwerke's Albatros CX. The AEG CIV was built almost completely of steel tubing and was powered by a 160-hp Mercedes DIII engine, while the Albatros CX was powered by a beefy 260 hp Mercedes CIVa engine, which gave it a maximum speed of 175 km/h/109mph. Some 300 of these were in service at the front by October 1917.

The Germans introduced a new type of aircraft, specially designed for the Schustas: the CL (light C-type). Instead of undertaking the usual C-type duties, the CL machines were to act as two-seater fighters and provide escort for C-class planes. Halberstädter

Flugzeug-Werke produced the first CL – the Halberstadt CLII. It was a small but strong two-seater – the pilot and observer sitting in a single cockpit – powered by a 160-hp Mercedes DIII engine. Coming into service in the summer of 1917, the Halberstadt CLII soon became very popular with the Schusta crews. At first each Schusta was allocated only two of these new aircraft. By 6 October the Fourth Army Schustas had aircraft as follows:

Halberstadt CL II	Schustas 7, 11, 13, 19, 30
LVG C V	Schustas 4, 10, 21
DFW C V	Schustas 16, 21

The Halberstadt was armed with one or two fixed Spandau machine-guns forward and one Parabellum machine-gun mounted on an elevated ring in the rear cockpit. Grenades could be carried in trays outside the fuselage and four or five 10-kg/22-lb bombs.

During summer 1917 the Germans brought another new type of plane into service – the J-type – which was specially designed for contact patrol missions in support of the infantry (J = I in Gothic German; I for Infanterieflieger – contact patrol plane). With semi-armoured fuselage the J-type was suited to its chief offensive role – that of harassing troops in the trenches from altitudes from 50 to 500 m/164 to 1640 ft.

In September 1917 FA (A) 250 at Heule was the first unit to receive the new J-type – the Junkers JI made by the Junkers Flugzeugwerke. The design of the new biplane was unorthodox with a very large upper wing, a small lower wing and a completely armoured nose. The 5-mm chrome-nickel sheet steel armour housed the 200-hp Benz engine and protected the cockpit. Although heavy and difficult to take off and land, the J1 was very robust and was well suited to its contact patrol duties – it flew low, was well armed and with its 5-mm armour, was difficult to shoot down.

The first, brand new, heavily armoured Junkers JI (J101/17) of Flieger-Abteilung (A) 250 at Heule, September 1917 (Collection Raven).

The airmen quickly dubbed it the *Möbelwagen* (furniture van) because of its size and the *Wellblechkiste* (corrugated steel-sheet box) because of its armour.

The D-type was developed specially for the Jastas. It was a fast and agile single-seater fighter biplane with two fixed Spandau machine-guns forward.

The new Albatros DIII, introduced in January 1917, was a copy of the Allies' Nieuport fighter. The DIII was powered by a 160- or 175-hp Mercedes DIIIa engine, giving it a maximum speed of 175 km/h/108 mph. It was the best of all the Albatros fighters and even when the DV model entered service the DIII continued in parallel production until early 1918. Despite its more powerful 175- or 185-hp Mercedes DIIIa engine and, consequently, slightly higher speed, the DV was not much of an improvement on the DIII. The other main difference was that the DV's fuselage was slightly

The Junkers JI at Heule airfield. The wings were made of a series of tubular duraluminium spars covered by a 2-mm skin. This superb but heavy aircraft needed a long airfield to take off and land (Collection Raven).

An Albatros DIII after a forced landing near Westrozebeke, November 1917. The DIII had a 160-hp Mercedes DIIIa engine; wingspan: 9.05 m/29 ft 8 in; length: 7.33 m/24 ft; loaded weight: 886 kg/1,949 lb; maximum speed: 165 km/h/108 mph (Collection Plane).

rounded while that of the DIII was flat. In October 1917 the DVa followed, but again it was not a significant improvement on the DIII.

One of the most successful and best-known single-seaters used by the German Jastas was the Fokker DrI triplane, built in the belief that three wings would give the aircraft greater manoeuvrability than a biplane. The British flew such an aircraft – the Sopwith Triplane – and the Germans pilots thought it was wonderful. The Fokker DrI with its 110-hp Oberursel rotary engine was a very agile plane and an effective weapon.

Anthony Fokker himself brought his two first DrIs to JG I at Marckebeke, demonstrated them to Manfred von Richthofen and his top aces, then left the two aircraft for them to take into action. They immediately proved their effectiveness. Manfred von Richthofen wrote a report:

1 September. Flying my triplane for the first time, I and four of my men of

Staffel 11 attacked a very courageously flown artillery plane. I approached and fired 20 rounds from a distance of 50 m/150 ft, whereupon the enemy fell out of control and crashed in our lines, near Zonnebeke. Apparently he had taken me for an English triplane, as the observer stood upright in the aircraft without making any move for his machine-gun.

Although they notched up over 20 victories, both prototypes had a short life. Oberleutnant Kurt Wolff in No 102/17 was shot down on 15 September, and Leutnant Werner Voss in No 103/17 was shot down and killed on September 23 after a long dogfight with seven aircraft of 56 Squadron RFC.

Following a series of fatal crashes the triplane was grounded in early November, but after the problems were resolved it came back into service during the last weeks of 1917. The Fokker DrI remained in service until the summer of 1918 although some pilots – notably Josef Jacobs, CO of Jasta

The funeral procession of Oberleutnant Wolff, St Joseph's Church, Courtrai, 18 September 1917. At the front of the procession is chief of the Fourth Army, Sixt von Arnim and to his left is Hauptmann Wilberg, Kofl or commander of the Fourth Army's flying units (Collection Raven).

Leutnant Werner Voss in his brand new Fokker triplane, ready for take-off, Marke airfield, late August 1917. The Dr1 was powered by a 110-hp Oberursel UR II engine; wingspan: 7.19 m/23 ft 7 in; length: 5.77 m/23 ft 7 in; loaded weight: 586 kg/1,289 lb; maximum speed 165 km/h/103 mph (own collection).

7, continued to fly that model until the armistice. It was in a triplane (No 425/17) that Germany's most famous ace, Manfred von Richthofen, was shot down on 21 April 1918.

The Big Brothers

Some 108 heavy bombers from three KGs were in action during the Third Battle of Ypres (31 July – 10 November 1917) – and

Gotha GIVs of KG 3 at Neumunster during the first raid on England . Because they guided the rest of the group bombers their fuselages were painted red. (Collection Kilduff USA).

A crashed Friedrichshafen GIII of Kasta 2 (KG 1), with pusher airscrew visible on the right engine, near Torhout in 1917 (Collection Raven).

one of them received additional orders – the bombing of London.

This was now possible because, at the end of 1916 Germany brought a new aircraft into service with a greatly increased range and bomb-load – the Gotha GIV. A new squadron was formed with 36 of these big aircraft, *Kampfgeschwader der Obersten Heeresleitung* (Army High Command heavy bomber squadron) Kagohl 3 or KG 3, under the command of Hauptmann Ernst Brandenburg. KG 3 consisted of six Kampfstaffeln (bomber squadrons) or Kastas (bombardment sections) which were based around Ghent: Kasta 13 and 14 at St-Denijs-Westrem, Kasta 15 and 16 at the airship base of Gontrode and Kasta 17 and

18 at Mariakerke. KG 3 was operational by mid-May, and on 25 May Brandenburg launched his first daylight attack against England, however they could not bomb the capital which was obscured by cloud, and the 21 aircraft dropped their bombs on targets near Ashford, Folkestone and Dover, killing 95 people. On the morning of 13 June 22 Gothas took off from Gontrode and St-Denijs-Westrem for the bloodiest air raid against London of the war. By the time the bombers turned for home no fewer than 162 people had been killed and 432 wounded, and England was thrown into panic.

The following day Brandenburg was invited to meet the Emperor to be awarded the Pour le Mérite, but unfortunately he was

seriously wounded when his plane crashed
on the flight back to the front from Germany.
Hauptmann Rudolf Kleine stepped into his
shoes.

Through July and August, Kleine sent his
bombers to targets in the south of England,
resulting in the deaths of 134 people, then on
the night of 3/4 September, Kleine launched
his first massive night bombing raid. During
the following months, KG 3 visited London
nine times, made numerous strikes against
strategic targets in southern England and
supported the Fourth Army by attacking
the French harbours of Dunkirk, Calais and
Boulogne.

The bomber unit KG 1 under command
of Hauptmann Alfred Keller was seconded

to the Fourth Army in June 1917. They flew Friedrichshafen GIIIs from their base at Ascq near Lille, and were the first to use 330 kg/660 lb bombs during a raid on St-Omer on 23 August. In mid-July KG 4, based at Kruishoutem near Wareghem, joined the fray.

The weekly report of 1-7 August 1917 details the activities of the bomber squadrons.

> *During the night KG1 dropped 3,900 kg/8,600 of bombs on artillery positions south of Ypres and north of Armentières. In a daytime raid KG 4 dropped 540 kg/1,120 lb of bombs on railways and airfields near Dunkirk, 1,560 kg/3,400 lb on camps and railways near Woesten and 570 kg/1,200 lb on batteries south of Ypres. Kasta 23, part of KG 3 but operating independently, dropped 750 kg/ 1,700 lb on bunkers west of Oost Dunkirk.*

These big birds needed protection in the crowded skies above Flanders:

> *16 August 1917. One Jasta of JG I had to fly escort for KG 1 from 1.00 pm during an attack on enemy batteries north of Zillebeke Lake.*

Even so, the bombers suffered heavy losses over Flanders. KG 1 lost Hauptmann Zorer, CO of Kasta 1, on 1 September, shot down by German friendly fire and taken prisoner by the British. Two days later Hauptmann Hempel, CO of KG 4, was made a POW. Hauptmann Rudolf Kleine, CO of KG 3, was killed during a bombing raid on Ypres on 12 December.

Despite these losses the German command continued to deploy their fleet of some 100 heavy bombers in the battle for Ypres because of their large bomb capacity – an FA could drop 150 kg/330 lb of bombs in a single sortie, while a KG could deliver 3,500 kg/7,700 lb.

Seven black and white Fokker triplanes from Jasta 26 on Menin-Ost during the Attack on Mount Kemmel. In the background a mill and the river Lys.

1918

The German Air Force in Early 1918

Throughout the winter of 1917 to 18 the air war continued, the sky filled with fierce confrontations every day – and the number of casualties grew. During January nine Jasta pilots were killed and a large number wounded, amounting to some ten per cent of the total strength of fighter pilots. Among the losses was Leutnant Max Müller, CO of Jasta 2. On 9 January, flying his Albatros DVa, he jumped a solitary RE8 reconnaissance plane. Afterwards the British crew reported:

While we were taking photographs of the area near Moorslede, we were attacked by seven enemy aircraft which approached from the north. One aircraft got to within 25 yards of our tail and the observer fired about 50 shots into it, and it turned off and burst into flames. It was last seen going down out of control and in flames between Dadizele and Moorslede.

The German command deployed a large number of flying units to wrest back aerial superiority over Flanders. On 26 January 1918 a report detailed the following units – probably some 180 aircraft:

There were 16 Flieger-Abteilungen: 3 (Thielt), 8 (Heule-Watermolen), 13 (Nachtegaal), 19 (St Denis-Westrem near Ghent), 26 (Meulebeke), 45B (Egem), (A) 211 (Erkegem near Oostcamp), 213 (Beveren), 221 (Bisseghem), 227 (Oostcamp), 231 (Ichtegem), 238

(Ingelmunster), 250 (Heule), 256 (Winghene), I Marine Feldflieger-Abteilung (Vlisseghem) and II Marine Feldflieger-Abteilung (Male near Bruges)

Reichenbildzug 2 under the command of Oberleutnant Fisser in Thielt

Seven Schustas: 1 (Heule-watermolen), 11 (Egem), 13 (Beveren), 23B (Ingelmunster), 26B (Erkegem), 28B (Ingelmunster) and 30B (Bisseghem)

Two Jagdgruppen (fighter groups): 3 (Winghene) and 4 (Bavikhove) and 12 Jastas: Boelcke (Bavikhove), 3 (Winghene), 7 (Wijnendale), 26 and 27 (Bavikhove), 28 (Varsenare), 36 (Cuerne), 37 (Winghene), 47 (Harlebeke), 51 (Winghene) and the two Marine Feld-Jastas (Koolkerke).

Seven Bostas* and one Riesenflugzeug-Abteilung** in the region around Ghent.

* After the reorganisation of the air force in 1917, Kasta units were renamed and became Bostas.

** Literally a 'giant' aircraft squadron. Flying huge Zeppelin Staaken RV1 aircraft, they were capable of carrying a bomb-load of 2,000 kg/4,400 lb.

During March some units left the Fourth Army in Flanders, so that by 21 March eleven FAs, seven Jastas and only one Schusta remained active in this sector – and this number continued to diminish.

Units as on 21 March 1918	Location
Marine Jagdgruppe	Koolkerke
I MFFA	Vlisseghem
II MFFA	Meetkerke
FA 19	Ichtegem
FA (A) 256	Winghene
Bostas 13 and 14	Mariakerke near Ghent
Bostas 15 and 16	Oostakker
Bosta 17	Gontrode
Bosta 18	Lemberge
FA 45	Egem
FA 3	Thielt
RBZ 2	Thielt
FA26	Meulebeke
Jasta 47	Beveren
Jasta 7	Rumbeke
FA 13	Nachtegaal
Jastas 28 and 51	Abele
Schusta 21	Ingelmunster
FA (A) 250	Heule
FA 8	Heule-Watermolen
Jasta 57	Belcamp (France)
FA 48	Wasquehal (France)

By this time the aircraft in service were, variously, the DFW CV, LVG CV and CVI, Rumpler CIV and CVII, Albatros JI, Junkers JI, Halberstadt CLII, Hannover CLII, Pfalz DIII, Albatros DIII, V and Va and the Fokker DrI.

The Hannover CLII was a new addition to the fighting force, introduced in December 1917. Designed specially for the Schustas, it was a small, compact plane, powered by a 180-hp Argus AsIII engine, with a single, centrally mounted Spandau machine-gun forward and a Parabellum machine-gun on a ring mounting for the observer. The observer had a better-than-usual field of fire to the rear because of the compact biplane tail.-

The Hannover and the Halberstadt formed the backbone of the German air attack on Mount Kemmel in late April 1918.

The Attack on Mount Kemmel

Towards the end of 1917 the German commanders Hindenburg and Ludendorff began to prepare for a major new offensive using reinforcements coming from the Russian front. Their aim was to make a decisive breakthrough and force the Allied command to sue for peace.

The first part of the German plan – an assault towards Amiens between 21 March and 4 April – failed. A second attack further north followed, and on 9 April the German Sixth Army overran the Portuguese-held lines between La Bassée and Armentières in France. Two days later, two Fourth Army reserve corps were brought into the attack on the small villages of Ploegsteert and Messines.

The Fourth Army had only a small air force at its disposal at the time of the attack:

The Fourth Army, April 1918		
Army High Command	Kofl 4 FA 3 and RBZ 2 Jagdgruppe 6 with Jastas 7, 28 and 51) BG 3	- Thielt (sometimes Zwevegem) Marke Ghent
Group North	Marine Kofl I MFFA II MFFA Marine Jagdgruppe	- Vlisseghem Ghistelles Jabbeke
Group Ypres	FA 26	Meulebeke
Group Wijtschate	FA (A) 250	Heule
Group Flanders	FA 13 FA (A) 256	Herseaux Neuville (F)

Flieger-Abteilung 26 and Schusta 28b at Meulebeke airfield with the take-off hut in the background, March 1918 (Collection Maertens).

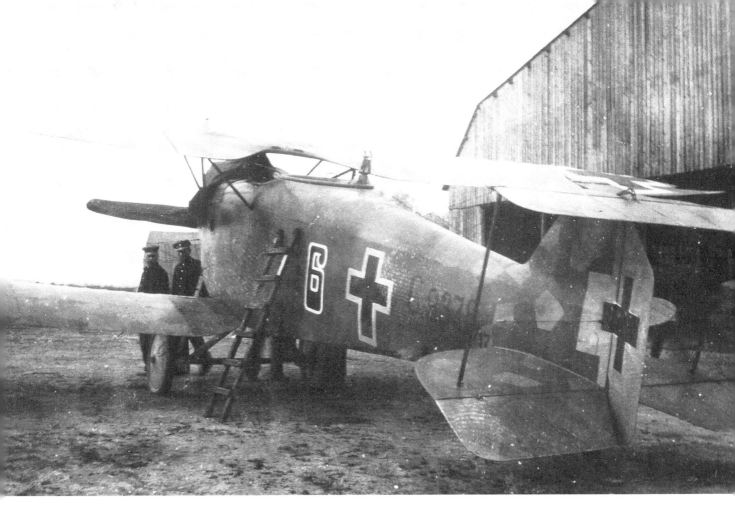

The Germans troops on the ground kept up the pressure on the Allied lines south of the Ypres Salient, as plans were made to double the drive to smash through the French and British and move towards the Channel coast. Mount Kemmel, a 149-m/450-ft hill, with its dominance over the Lys valley was of considerable tactical importance, and the heavily fortified hill became a key objective in the forthcoming offensive.

In early April troops and equipment started moving north, and there remained the possibility that the Allied reconnaissance aircraft might uncover the German master-plan. To minimise this risk, all movement of troops and materiel was done by night and the guns and men were carefully hidden during the day. These nocturnal transfers were hampered by bad weather and overcrowding on the troop transport trains, all of which delayed the overall German build-up, but from 12 April the Fourth Army got following reinforcements:

XVIII Reserve Corps	FA (A) 221 and 233 (both at Moorsele) FA (A) 204 (Menin-Coucou) Grufl 3
X Reserve Corps	FA(A) 258 and 266 (Linselles)
Group Ypres	Grufl 1 FA(A) 240 and 288 (both on Beveren-Roulers) Jagdgruppe 9
Army High Command	Jastas 3, 16B and 54 (Ingelmunster) Jasta 56 (Bisseghem) Schlastas 10, 23, 26 and 30B (Bisseghem) Schlastas 1, 14 and 28 (Heule)

During the battle for Mount Kemmel FA 26 was the sole unit flying for Group Ypres. The photo shows one of their workhorses at Meulebeke airfield – a Hannover CL-II (C 9378/17), with its typical biplane tail. The Maltese Cross originally on the fin has been altered to the new Balkenkreuz design, which dates the photo around April 1918.

Power plant: a single 180-hp Argus AS III 6 cylinder in-line water-cooled engine; wingspan: 11.7 m/38 ft 4 in; length: 7.58 m/24 ft 10 in; height: 2.8 m/9 ft 2 in; maximum speed: 165 km/h/103.12 mph at 5,000 m/15,000 ft; armament: one machine-gun forward and one manually operated by the observer (Collection Maertens).

The completely ruined landscape made orientation very difficult for the aircrews:

10 April 1918. Patrol by Leutnant Strähle, Vizefeldwebel Wieprich and Gefreiter Hitschler (all of Jasta 57). It was very exciting flying at low level in our Albatros DVs – we could make out every man below, although finding our way was very difficult. There were many columns of troops on the roads, and balloons made flying dangerous. We saw wounded being carried away. The Lys bridges had been blown up. There was no enemy activity in the air owing to the bad weather.

In spite of the hazards caused by bad weather the FAs continued their sorties. Day after day they directed the artillery and searched the ground for their own and enemy troops, as described in a FA (A) 221 report:

What Schlastas and Infanterieflieger do these days is incredible. They are the only people who can find their way over this destroyed landscape, which is devoid of any point of orientation!

The Allies shot down many of these low-flying planes – between 10 and 17 April six aircraft were shot down and many others had to make emergency landings or returned home damaged.

The Jastas kept up their aggressive role. Leutnant Jacobs of Jasta 7 reported:

12 April. Around 6.15 am, we started our first patrol of the day. We sighted seven SEs, which we attacked immediately. I manoeuvred into a very good firing position to strike one of them, but he did not fall. A little later we attacked four Bristol two-seaters – which disappeared. During this attack my aircraft took a burst of machine-gun fire, then the enemy flak scored a hit

Emil and Franz with their Halberstadt CLII at Bisseghem. Emil and Franz were nicknames for the occupants of German two-seater aircraft, 'Emil' being the pilot, and 'Franz' the observer. The external rack carries flares and signalling pistol and the elevated gun-ring allows the observer to fire both up and downwards (Collection Haerynck Belgium).

on my propeller and it stopped. We got home around 7.25 am, but then took off twice more but without incident. On our last flight Leutnant Lotz shot down an Armstrong-Whitworth over Bailleul airfield. Flights over the front 9.15-10.40 am and 4.05-5.15 pm.

Everywhere we could see burning villages and fighting in the streets and fields. We have advanced a long way and are now in front of Bailleul. Armentières has been captured.

During the night of 12/13 April BG 3 dropped 11,800 kg/26,000 lb of bombs on St-Omer and Hazebrouck.

On 15 April the German Sixth Army took Bailleul and captured two British airfields. Leutnant Strähle (Jasta 57) was one of the first visitors:

We made a landing at the British aerodrome at la Gorgue near Estaires and found a lot of fuel there. On the field were the burnt remains of about a dozen Camels, which they had destroyed before retreating.

Crews of the FAs supported the German advances. FA (A) 221 reported:

18 April 1918. Low clouds, very showery and very strong wind. Between 1.30 and 2.15 pm observer Leutnant Walther reported very heavy enemy presence in the craters in front of the 7th Infantry Division. Heavy anti-aircraft fire prevented us from looking into their trenches. There were some 20 men to a crater-hole. We expect an attack between Wijtschate and Rondellwald. The crew dropped a message near Division Headquarters and a heavy shelling of the enemy positions began.

On the evening of 18 April, FA (A) 250 managed to locate the new British battery positions and over the course of the next few days the reconnaissance units reported a heavy build-up of enemy activity between the Black and Red Mountains.

Strong German pressure forced the Allies to withdraw to new positions nearer to Ypres, leaving all the territory they had gained the previous year. The only flying unit of Group Ypres, FA 26, observed the British withdrawal closely. Three of its crews transmitted details of all enemy movements and two other teams made surveillance sorties above the Allied supply lines, army camps and dumps, ranging the artillery fire on any suspicious enemy movement and making bombing raids. A sixth crew of FA 26 remained on stand-by.

Wilberg, Kofl of the Fourth Army, grouped his flying units to increase the German airpower, creating the following groups:

Jagdgruppe 3 consisting of Jastas 20, 33, 40, 49, 57 and 58

Jagdgruppe 6 consisting of Jastas 7, 16, 28, 47 and 51

Jagdgruppe 9 consisting of Jastas 3, 54 and 56

JG 3, with the elite Jastas 2, 26, 27 and 36, was brought in to support these groups, and emergency landing strips were laid north of Ghits, west of St Eloois-Winkel and north of Menin in preparation for the forthcoming attack.

Wilberg also created large formations – *Schlachtgeschwadern* (battle group or wings), made up of *Schlachtstaffeln* (battle squadrons) or Schlastas, which replaced the Schustas:

Schlachtgeschwader A: Schlastas 1, 14, 21 and 28 flying from Heule

Schlachtgeschwader B: Schlastas 10, 23B, 26 and 30B, concentrated on Bisseghem airfield

Schlachtgeschwader C: Schlastas 3, 13, 19 and 29, at Ingelmunster

Schlachtgeschwader D: Schlastas 9, 12, 16 and 24B, based at Linselles in France

The battle opened on the morning of 25 April as the German artillery began shelling the British defences with gas grenades. Finally at 5 am the infantry stormed the enemy positions, with XVIII Reserve Corps capturing the village of Kemmel and the Bavarian mountain troops of X Reserve Corps taking Mount Kemmel itself.

Four formations of low-flying ground-attack planes set off simultaneously from the south, heading for the enemy positions. Some 80 aircraft of the four battle groups attacked in two waves. To achieve total surprise, the first wave raided the enemy trenches five minutes after the start of the ground attack. The second wave came in shortly afterwards, attacking the Allied batteries and reinforcements.

For the rest of the day the Schlastas took it in turn to fly two-hour sorties above the lines.

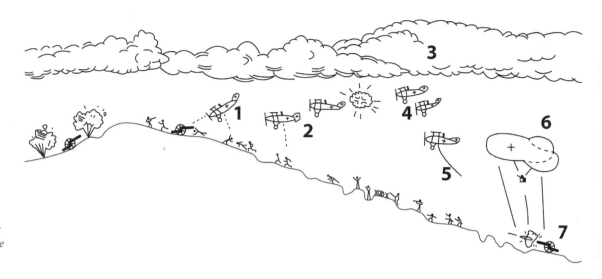

The FAs were also operating in that airspace as, flying just below the clouds, they worked in co-operation with the infantry and artillery. At higher levels the Jastas fought a grim battle to protect the reconnaissance and bomber aircraft.

On 29 April Germany launched another mass attack to clear the way to Poperinghe. The battle opened early in the morning, with the artillery pouring thousands of gas grenades on to the Allied batteries. The previous evening Leutnant Friedrich Nielebock, an observer of FA (A) 250, had located most of the new Allied artillery positions, for which he was awarded the Pour le Mérite.

To support the infantry assault, waves of bombers were to strike the Allied positions between Dikkebus and Reningelst. However, heavy anti-aircraft fire damaged most of the 48 planes of the Schlachtgeschwadern B and D supporting X Reserve Corps, rendering 17 planes unserviceable.

The Jastas came up against even heavier resistance. During one of the dogfights, flying ace Leutnant Bongartz of Jasta 36, flying a Fokker triplane, was hit in the head, lost his left eye and crashed near Ploegsteert at 1.00 pm. He was one of that day's victims downed by Captain Mick Mannock's No 74 Squadron of what was now the Royal Air Force.

By evening battle was over – the German drive to break through the Allied lines and take the hills south of Ypres had failed badly.

Summer 1918 – Increasing Allied Pressure

May 1918 was one of the bloodiest months of the war for the German air force in Flanders. At least 40 airmen – about ten per cent of the strength of pilots and observers – were killed. It wasn't until the end of May that the Allied pressure eased enough to allow the German command to transfer most of the flying units to other armies. On 23 May JG III left Flanders, then in the first weeks of June FA (A) 221, 240, 213 and FA 45 followed, until by mid-June only a small air fleet remained:

FA 3 with RBZ 2 at Bisseghem
FA 8 in the Lille region
FA 13 at Linselles or Herseaux
FA 19 in northern France
FA 26 at Beveren-Roulers
FA 48 in Northern France
FA (A) 204 at Halluin
FA (A) 213 in northern France
FA (A) 250 at Bisseghem or Menin-Coucou
FA (A) 256, 258 and 266 in northern France
F (A) 288 at Beveren-Roulers
Schlasta 16 at Stalhille

Schlastas 9, 12, 24 and 25 in northern
  France
Jagdgruppe 9 with Jastas 7 and 16 at St-
  Marguerite (Comines) in France, Jasta
  20 at Menin, Jasta 40 at Lomme (near
  Lille in France) in France and Jastas 51
  and 56 at Rumbeke

The Fourth Army still had support
from BG 3 with its six squadrons of heavy
bombers and, from 7 May onwards, the three
Zeppelin Staaken RVIs of *Riesenflugzeug
Abteilung* 501, based at Scheldewindeke.
These massive aircraft could easily carry a
bomb-load of 2,000 kg/4,400 lb.

The advances that Germany had made
during April allowed the Fourth Army to
move most of its flying units forward to
bases south of the River Lys, on French
soil. The previously abandoned airfields of
Menin-Coucou and Moorsele now came
back into use and a new airfield was cleared
in the northern suburbs of Menin. From
1 June the Bisseghem airfield was home
to a *Vorpark* (advanced section) of AFP 4

from Ghent, and here the Schlastas and FAs
could be supplied with new C-type planes,
ammunition and photographic equipment.

The initial five Schlastas (from August
only two – Schlastas 9 and 16) were
increasingly used as interceptors against
night bombing raids. Almost every day great
swarms of Allied aircraft crossed the lines
and bombed strategic German targets, and
the five Jastas of the Marine Jagdgruppe and
Jagdgruppe 9 put up a spirited fight against
them, as Carl Degelow, CO of Jasta 40,
recalled in his war memoir:

> On 14 July our squadron had taken off
> on an evening patrol. From experience,
> we knew that the English bomber
> squadrons advanced across our lines at
> that time... That evening our six aircraft
> brought down four SE-5 fighters.

In April 1918 the Jastas received their first
Fokker DVIIs, which became without doubt
the most famous of the German fighters of
WWI. The Fokker DVII was a product of the

first competition to create a D-class aircraft and proved to be superior to all other entries. Initially the DVII was fitted with a 160-hp Mercedes DIII engine, then later with the new, more powerful 185-hp BMW, giving a much-improved performance.

The DVII's main advantage over other German fighter planes was its ability to maintain good performance at high altitude, and it could also 'hang on its prop' allowing the guns to be trained on an enemy aircraft at higher altitude. Throughout the summer of 1918 increasing numbers of these agile machines came into operation. Jastas 7 and 56 received their DVIIs in June, Jasta 40 and I Marine Jasta in July, II Marine Jasta from 13 July and the DVII finally reached the Seefrosta on 19 August.

Leutnant der Reserve Willy Thöne of I Marine Feldjagdstaffel, encountered a tough opponent on 31 July:

My opponent must have been pretty important, as his plane carried three pennants. Our dogfight had already gone on for 15 minutes and in that time we had come down to about 20 m/60 ft. Then my Englishman put on full throttle and flew to the west at about 10-20 m/30-60 ft, trying to escape towards his lines. We passed very low over the cornfields, houses and grasslands, almost grazing the heads of wheat. When he went to straighten up, I fired a few rounds with my two guns. Now we were flying above the flooded Yser area, and still I followed him at low level – but my pursuit was not without problems. One moment I held him in my sight without being able to down him, the next my gun jammed and I had to fix the problem. I now was rather close behind him and we were back flying over dry land. I fired for the umpteenth time and suddenly he flew into the ground. I was about 5 km/3 miles inside enemy lines and flying at only 20 m/60 ft. I pulled up and returned home...

During my homeward flight I was shot down by Belgian anti-aircraft fire

Fokker DVII with a four-color Lozenge-Tarnung (lozenge camouflage) in Belgian colors shortly after the end of war (own collection).

and overturned on the flooded east-bank of the Yser River. My plane was destroyed but I managed to reach our own lines by wading through the water.

The DVII proved very effective and finally swayed the balance, giving Germany aerial superiority, and the German High Command decided to hold another competition to design a single-seater fighter. Again it was a Fokker that beat the other entries – this time a parasol monoplane with a 110-hp Oberursel UII 9 rotary engine. Initially 400 were ordered with the *Eindecker* (monoplane) designation EV, and early in June the Naval Jastas and specialised *Seefrontstaffeln* (coastal protection squadrons) or Seefrostas received the new aircraft.

After three serious crashes due to wing failure the EV was redesigned and renamed as the DVIII, and new models began to reach

the front towards the end of October. Only 58 were in operation by 1 November to demonstrate their manoeuvrability.

Despite having these superior aircraft, the German aircrews lost the upper hand over the battlefields, and they could only regain temporary control in certain sectors by throwing large formations of Jastas or Schlastas into the battle.

On the other side, the Allies, now with support from the USA, gained in strength both on the ground and in the sky. The German High Command realised that it was only a matter of time before the Allies would launch a decisive offensive.

The Naval Corps' Last Year in Flanders

The last 12 months of the war saw the birth of a number of new flying units within the Naval Corps. On 1 October 1917 the

Commandeur der Landflieger (Chief of the land-based flying units of the Marine Corps) had created the *Seefrontstaffel* or Seefrosta (squadron for coastal protection) at Neumunster under Leutnant zur See Hans Rolshoven, formerly of the II MLFA. Its 15 Albatros DIIIs, which had flotation bags inside the fuselage, were tasked with protecting the slow seaplanes of the Naval Corps.

The unit became operational on the 21 October, making two sorties to Dunkirk and Gravelines on the French coast, and a week later the unit consisted of just nine pilots. Originally intended as a major unit similar to a Jasta with 13-15 pilots, the Seefrosta was constantly undermanned, and most of the time the unit had only six pilots available for its 13 aircraft.

The unit's war diary describes their first important patrol:

28 October: one group of four and a further group of two aircraft flew escort for a bombing raid by the seaplanes based at Zeebruges from 4.45 to 6.10 am and from 5.10 to 5.35 am. The first group also carried out reconnaissance along the French coast.

On 31 October, aircraft of the Seefrosta appeared for the first time over the English coast.

On 6 May 1918 the unit suffered a major setback when its commander, Leutnant zur See Rolshoven crashed.

At 3.30 pm Leutnant zur See Rolshoven flew to Zeebruges and landed on the beach near the mole. After talks with the leading officers of the Naval Air Station he took off but crashed from a height of 300 m/1,000 ft for no apparent reason.

The Albatros DIII of Leutnant Blum of Jasta 57, spring 1918, above the Ypres Salient. The plane is marked with a Balkenkreuz – a stylised version of the Iron Cross – from July 1918 the German national crest changed to a narrower cross design (Collection Maertens).

He was buried at Zeebruges and Leutnant zur See Poss took command of the unit.

On 1 August 1918 the unit split into Seefrosta 1 and Seefrosta 2 (this latter being smaller with only about eight aircraft), based in the neighbouring villages of Neumunster and Vlisseghem.

These units gradually got new and better aircraft:

11 November 1917	Pfalz D III
16 March 1918	Albatros DVa and Halberstadt CLII
5 August 1918	Fokker DVII
12 August 1918	Fokker EV

On 5 August 1918 the Seefrostas had the following aircraft:

	Seefrosta 1	Seefrosta 2
Albatros DVa	3	0
Fokker DVII	7	5
not operational	5	2

One of the most dangerous tasks of the Seefrosta was the protection of the incoming and outgoing submarines during their passage through the long canals between Bruges and the seaports of Zeebruges and Ostend.

By the first of September the two Seefrostas became the IV and V Marine Feldjagdstaffel. At that time they had scored 28 victories and suffered three losses.

Since November 1914 Germany had installed more than 30 batteries along the coastline with over 120 guns to counter bombardment from Allied vessels in the Channel and prevent Allied landings on the Belgian coast. The coastal squadrons not only had to protect the seaplanes but also the impressive array of batteries along the Belgian coast, and for this another type of squadron was created – the *Küstenflieger-Abteilungen* (coastal flying squadrons), or Küstas, which would direct these batteries' fire.

Originally the German command intended to provide each battery with its own artillery support aircraft – a seaplane from Zeebruges available at the battery commander's disposal. However, it was not viable for every battery to have its own plane, so there was a change in how aerial reconnaissance was organised. At the beginning of 1917 two coastal air units had

Hansa-Brandenburg W12s, Nos 1408 and 2004, of the Imperial German Navy at Zeebruges. Both are of the C2MG version with machine-gun packed against the rain and open cockpit door (Collection Plane).

Hansa-Brandenburg W12, No 2124, with two different styles of national marking, which date this picture around April 1918 (own collection).

been established at the seaplane bases of Zeebruges and Ostend, which became the eyes of the naval guns. On 17 September 1917 these two Küstas were redesignated as the *Küstenflieger-Abteilung Flandern* (Flanders coastal flying squadron).

Every time Allied ships shelled the coast or harbours, the Küsta seaplanes took off and ranged their own guns against the aggressors. This was a difficult challenge for these slow floatplanes, especially as they were no match for the agile land-based aircraft which protected the Allied ships. It was a hard and risky work as the war diary recorded:

22 September. A rainy day with a south-westerly wind. Three Friedrichshafen FF33L seaplanes on reconnaissance between 6.00 and 7.15 am. Shortly after the start, number 1276 crashes from low altitude. The plane is totally wrecked. The crew, pilot Flugmeister Verreiter and observer Oberleutnant der Reserve Schatz are slightly injured. Seaplane 1089 found an enemy monitor and 14 destroyers heading to the east in quadrant 058b. [The Germans had divided the North Sea into equal squares that were identified with numbers and letters.]

8.00 - 9.30 am two artillery support aircraft took off after receiving a report that vessels in quadrant 059b were bombarding Ostend. The crew of seaplane 1089, observer Vizefeuerwerker Ruhräh and pilot Flugobermaat Steinitz reported an enemy monitor in quadrant 059b at 8.29 am. Land-based English fighters attacked the seaplane immediately. Another of our pilots found plane No 1089 floating on the waves. It was impossible to rescue the crew due to the presence of English fighters in the vicinity. Later plane No 1159 saw an enemy destroyer picking up the crew.

The naval command now decided to give the Küsta seaplanes an escort of land-based planes from the *Marine Schutzstaffel* (naval protection squadron). On 23 September this squadron moved to Neumunster with three Albatros C VIIIs and three DFWs, and from this time artillery-spotting seaplanes flew only under their protection.

17 October. 7.16 - 8.50 am, two artillery and three escort aircraft made a patrol along the Belgian coast. No blockade ships were found. At the Thortonbank a Sopwith and two Spads attacked both seaplanes. The crew of FF33 No 1240 was hit but both aircraft managed to return safely to their base at Ostend.

16 March 1918. 10.40 - 11.40 am, two Küsta aircraft and three Schusta aircraft took off for a reconnaissance-flight. They found one monitor, six destroyers, three torpedo boats and many motorboats in the area 066b and 065b. They were steaming in an easterly direction. The Deutschland coastal battery requested one of our crews but unfortunately our aircraft could not help direct and find range for their guns as they were driven off by eight enemy aircraft.

The coastal flying units were also used to protect the experimental Fernlenkboot (FL) – a kind of unmanned torpedo with an explosive warhead, which travelled over the surface of coastal waters, controlled by an electric cable.

28 October 1917. 1.00 - 3.00 pm. Three artillery and three escort planes patrolled with the FL boat in quadrant 066 and 059b. In area 066 they found one monitor, eight destroyers and a lot

of motorboats. The FL boat scored a hit on the monitor. The damaged vessel took on water and explosions were seen on board. Plane No 1240 called in fire from the Tirpitz coastal battery on to the monitor, at which the battery responded: 'Battery will not shoot'.

In the last months of 1917 and through 1918 the Marine Schutzstaffeln and Küstenflieger-Abteilungen grew in number. Küsta 3 was formed at the end of 1917 and Küsta 4 in April 1918, both of which flew

land-based planes. Marine Schusta 2 became operational in March or April 1918.

Küsta 1 at Zeebruges and Küsta 2 at Ostend flew a mixture of Friedrichshafen FF33L, FF49c and Brandenburg W12 seaplanes. The other units each had six LVG CV land-based planes and flew from Uitkerke.

On 23 April the harbour and seaplane base at Zeebruges took a beating when British commandos attacked the mole, also sinking three old ships at the narrowest point of the harbour, so blocking the exit of

the Bruges-Zeebruges canal into the sea. In the course of the raid a British submarine destroyed the entrance to the mole, so that the seaplanes could no longer reach the Zeebruges seaplane base by rail, however, the German command solved the problem by sending their planes into the water off the beach at Zeebruges.

On 3 April 1918 the two Jastas of the Marine Jagdgruppe moved from Koolkerke to Jabbeke, some 16 km/10 miles west of Bruges, where they stayed for the last months of the war. It was in May that Marine Jagdgruppe scored its hundredth victory.

Due to continuous Allied bombing raids over the coastal region, the naval corps command formed a third Marine Marinefeldjagdstaffel on 23 June, under command of Leutnant zur See Brockhoff. The Marine Jagdgruppe's difficulty in preventing the enemy's daily attacks on the U-boat installations at Bruges, Zeebruges and Ostend prompted the naval fighter pilots to adopt a new tactic. As soon as an enemy squadron was reported heading for Bruges, the naval Jastas positioned themselves above the front line, blocking the enemy's route home … and this tactic proved effective almost immediately.

12 August 1918. Vizeflugmeister Thöne downed a Spad near Poelkapelle and another one over the sea near Wenduine. Leutnant zur See Sachsenberg scored two victories: a Sopwith single-seater near Ostend and, two minutes later, a de Havilland. Both aircraft fell into the sea. All victories were later confirmed.

It wasn't long before the Allies retaliated. When reconnaissance showed that the German fighter squadrons were operating from an airfield at Varsenare, this became a prime target. On 13 August at 6.30 am, Allied aircraft raided the naval Jastas' base. Some 70 British and American Camels, followed by DH 4s bombed and attacked the airfield

for 15 minutes, flying almost at ground level. The château and nine of II Marinefeldjasta's Fokker DVIIs were destroyed.

On 1 September 1918 two new Marinefeldjagdstaffeln were created to operate from Neumunster – Marinefeld-jagdstaffel IV under the command of Leutnant zur See Reinhold Poss and Marinefeldjagdstaffel V under Leutnant zur See Paul Achilles. The Marine Jagdgruppe was renamed as the *Marinejagdgeschwader* (naval fighter squadron) under CO Sachsenberg and Leutnant zur See Philip Becht took command of Marine Jasta I. When Poss was shot down and taken prisoner on 15 October, Leutnant zur See Eberhard Krantz took over Marine Jasta IV. The naval fighter squadron ended the war with at least 230 victories – but at the cost of 32 pilots killed.

Airfields in 1917 and 1918

The Germans built more than 30 new airfields in Flanders during 1917, which played an important role in the Third Battle for Ypres, which lasted from August until the end of November.

Prerequisites for locating these airfields were well-drained, sandy and quick-drying ground, a railway station within easy reach, a château and a local village. The station meant easy supply of materials and direct phone and telegraph connections, the château or the houses of the bourgeoisie would provide accommodation for the officers and the men could find billets among the civilian population and farmers. The many canals, so typical of the Flemish countryside, were boarded over with wood and most of the tents, sheds and hangars were located among farm buildings or along a row of trees to disguise the aerodrome against aerial observation.

Aartrijke
This village located some 6 km/3.6 miles north-west of Torhout, had two airfields, the

first near the rest home and nunnery (NU) just outside the village and the second was in the south-west corner of the village near the château about 3 km/2 miles outside the village. This field was named *Sparappelhoek* – Pine-cone Corner.

Units	Period
Marinefeldjagdstaffel 1	4 April -10 September 1917 (NU)
FA (A) 231	End May -13 September 1917
	20 December 1917-21 February 1918
Schutzstaffel (see below) 10	18 July -18 September 1917
FA (A) 264	31 October - 25 November 1917
Jasta 7 (SP)	15 September 1917-1 March 1918
Jasta 29	14 September - 28 November 1917
	5 October -11 November 1918
Jasta 35	18 September -1 December 1917 (NU)
Jasta 51	circa January -1 March 1918
Jasta 16	7 February -14 March 1918
Js 14	last month of occupation

A bombing raid on Aartrijke airfield, winter 1917, when a bomb damaged the adjacent nunnery (own collection).

Bavikhove-Abeelhoek

Bavikhove, just to the north of Harlebeke, had two airfields. The first, Abeelhoek, was located some 2 km/1.5 miles to the west of the small village near Cuerne.

Units	Period of occupation
FA 8	31 May - 15 September 1917
Jasta 11	10 June - 1 July 1917
Jasta 31	15 June - 1 September 1917
Jasta 18	2 July - 23 November 1917
Jasta 24	8 September - 23 November 1917

Bavikhove (east side, just outside the village along the Hogestraat-Ooigem road)

Units	Period of occupation
Jasta 27	1 November 1917 - 10 February 1918
Jasta 26	2 November 1917 - 13 February 1918

The following units were based on one of the two Bavikhove airfields:

Units	Period of occupation
Jasta 2	13 November 1917 - 16 February 1918
Jasta 23	23 September - 16 October 1917

Beveren

This airfield was active until end of occupation in mid-October 1918.

Units	Period of occupation
FA (A) 213	November 1916 - 10 March 1918
FA(A)240	11 April 1918 – mid May 1918
FA (A) 288	circa April 1918 - end of occupation
FA 26	Summer 1918 - end of occupation
Schutzstaffel *(Schusta) 13	circa 2 June 1917 - 21 February 1918
Jasta 47	8 March - 29 March 1918

* These escort/protection squadrons were formed early in 1917 from dismantled KAGOHLs.

Bisseghem

This field was built during the second half of 1916 between the villages of Wevelghem and Bisseghem on the Courtrai-Menin road, about 4 km/2.5 miles from Courtrai.

Units	Period of occupation
FA 6	9 February – c May 1917
FA 3	early 1917 - 23 November 1917
	17 April 1918
FA (A) 221	9 May 1917 -10 March 1918
Schusta 4	9 June - 24 August 1917
Schusta 30	9 June 1917 - February/March 1918
	12 April 1918 (short stay)
Jasta 6	10 June - 24 November 1917
Schusta 12	18 July - 11 September 1917
Schlachtstaffel (Schlasta) 10	12 April 1918 (short stay)
Schlasta 23	12 April 1918 (short stay)
Schlasta 26	12 April 1918 (short stay)
FA (A) 250	7 June 1918 – end of occupation
Jasta 40	28 September - 8 October 1918

Cuerne

Cuerne is located just north east of Courtrai. This field was an extension to the aerodromes of Heule.

Units	Period of occupation
Jasta 4	27 June - 1 July 1917
Jasta 36	2 July 1917 - 11 March 1918

Desselgem

This village had two airfields. The construction of the first, Flugplatz Ooigem, began on 21 July 1917. A few days later a second field, Desselgem Dries, was prepared.

Units	Period of occupation
FA 8	Mid September - end October 1917
FA 13	27 October - end November 1917
FA 25	July - 15 November 1917
Schusta 25	13 July - 15 November 1917

Egem

The airfield was about 9 km/5 miles north-east of Roulers at the right-hand side of the main Courtrai-Bruges road. An eyewitness described the construction in a diary:

Aerial view of Ooigem airfield at Desselgem near the River Lys. (Collection Maertens).

3 June 1917. Two lorries arrived with materials for building and all able-bodied men had to help with the construction.

The following day some six large tents were erected. The aerodrome had a surface area of 9 hectares. On Thursday 14 June some 400 men of the Saxon Army arrived from Douai in France. Throughout the day many cars and lorries brought material in. On Saturday 16 June the first six aircraft landed. The following day another six arrived, one of which turned over on landing. The wireless station was located in a pub.

Units	Period of occupation
FA 45	circa 9 June 1917 - 26 March 1918
FA (A) 238	September 1917
Schusta 11	October 1917 – January 1918
Schusta 12	September 1917
Schusta 13	Mid-December 1917

Handzame

This was one of the first German aerodromes in Flanders but had to be abandoned in July 1917 due to heavy shelling.

Units	Period of occupation
FFA 19	End January 1917 - July 1917
FFA 48	Beginning of summer 1917 (short stay)
Jasta 29	18 July - 1 August 1917

Heule

This village is located just north of Courtrai. The airfield got two names: the part in the west was named Heule, the part in the east was named Heule Watermolen (watermill).

Units	Period of occupation
FA 6	April - May 1917
FA (A) 250	May 1917 - March 1918
Jasta 10	25 June - 2 July 1917
Jasta 24	26 June - 8 September 1917
Schusta 6	June - November 1917
Schusta 17	Summer - 15 November 1917
Schusta 24	Summer - 8 November 1917
Schusta 1	20 December 1917 - summer 1918
Schlastas 1, 14, 21 and 28 B	Mid-April 1918
Schusta 14	circa 21 April 1918
Schusta 21	circa 21 April 1918

Ichtegem

The airfield was built near a small village about 7 km/4.5 miles north-west of Torhout.

Units	Period of occupation
Schusta 16	circa June - 15 November 1917
Jasta 35	21 July -18 July 1917
Jasta 33	23 July - 15 September 1917
Schusta 10	18 September - 27 November 1917
Schusta 5	31 October – 25 November 1917

Ingelmunster

This small town is some 10 km/6 miles north of Courtrai. There were two aerodromes, the first built in January 1917, south-west of the village and south of the road to Iseghem (R in the table), not far away from the château. The second, built in May 1917, was about 1 km/0.6 mile north-east of Ingelmunster itself, near the neighbouring village of Meulebeke (M in the table).

Units	Period of occupation
FA(A)224	9 February 1917 - 3 April 1918 on R
FA 26	Summer 1917 – 27 October 1917 on R Mid July 1917 – early Summer 1918 on M
FA 7	Summer 1917 – 29 August 1917
FA 19	Summer 1917 – 27 October 1917 on R
Schusta 23B	August 1917 – March 1918 on R
Schusta 28B	28 August 1917 – March 1918 on R
FA(A)238	October 1917 – 10 February 1918
Schusta 19	Summer 1917
Schusta 9	27 October 1917 – 24 November 1917
Jasta 3	11 April 1918 – 4 May 1918
Jasta 54	11 April 1918 – 4 May 1918
Jasta 56	11 April 1918 –5 May 1918

(Bottom right)
An aerial view of Ichtegem airfield (own collection).

(Bottom left)
Hangars of Flieger-Abteilung (A) 250 at Heule, summer 1917. In the background are the tents of Jasta 10 or 24 (Collection Raven).

Iseghem

The small industrial town of Iseghem was located about 6.5 km/4 miles to south-east of Roulers. This field, also known as Abele, was the continuation of Rumbeke-Ost and built at the same time.

Units	Period of occupation
Schusta 2	circa 9 June - c 16 June 1917
Jasta 26	16 June - 1 November 1917
Jasta 27	16 June - 31 October 1917
FA 19 (?)	circa July 1917
FA (A) 213	2 February - 9 March 1918
Jasta 51	1 March - 23 April 1918
Jasta 28	8 March - 6 June 1918
FA (A) 221	6 May - 1 June 1918

Jabbeke

Jabbeke was situated about 6.5 km/4 miles south-west of Bruges. The airfield itself was built on farmland near the château outside the village.

Units	Period of occupation
FA (A) 293 B	26 May - July/August 1917
Marinefeldflieger-Abteilung	12 July - 22 August 1917
FA (A) 233	18 July - 24 August 1917
Marine Schusta I	Summer 1917
Jasta 28	27 August 1917 - 31 January 1918
Jasta 20	31 August - 23 November 1917
Marine Jasta 1	3 April - c 25 August 1918
Marine Jasta 2	3 April 1918 - end of occupation
Marine Jasta 3	23 June 1918 - end of occupation
Marine Jasta 4	1 September 1918 - end of occupation
Marine Jasta 5	1 September 1918 - end of occupation

Koolkerke

The aerodrome was built to house the Marine Jagdstaffel, tasked with protecting the harbour at Bruges. The aerodrome itself was about 1.6 km/1 mile north of the harbour on the left side of the Bruges-Zeebruges canal.

The take-off hut at Ingelmunster aerodrome, as in 2010. See illustration p 136 (own collection).

An aerial view of
Marckebeke airfield, its tents
set up around the central
farm. We can see a line-up of
planes near the park of the
château. To the north of the
River Lys lies the village of
Bisseghem, the hangars of
which airfield are visible on
the road upper left. In the
lower right corner is Courtrai
railway station (own
collection).

Units	Period of occupation
I Marinefeldjagdstaffel	10 September 1917 - early April 1918
II Marinefeldjagdstaffel	19 October 1917 - 3 April 1918
KG 1	End August 1917

Lichtervelde

This airfield occupied the junction of the Bruges-Courtrai and Ghent-Dixmude railways.

Units	Period of occupation
FA (A) 256	circa 2 June - 24 August 1917

Marke

Marke was a small village just south west of Courtrai and had two airfields. The first field was constructed during January 1917 to the north-east of the village. On 30 July the ace Werner Voss arrived to take permanent command of Jasta 10 in von Richthofen's Jagdgeschwader 1 (JG 1), or 'the Flying Circus' as it was dubbed by the Allied airmen.

Units	Period of occupation
Jasta 28	24 January - 25 March 1917
FA 3	April 1917
Jasta 10	2 July - 24 November 1917
Jasta 2	16 February - 15 March 1918

The second airfield, Marckebeke was built during spring 1917 near the Château de Béthune just south of the River Lys, and was separated from the first airfield by the Courtrai-Lille railway line. It was home to the 'Flying Circus' and to many famous German aces – the brothers von Richthofen, Goering and Loerzer.

Units	Period of occupation
Jasta 18	16 June - 2 July 1917
Jasta 36	27 June - 2 July 1917
Jasta 4	2 July - 21 November 1917
Jasta 11	2 July - 24 November 1917
F.T.-Versuchs-Abteilung Döberitz*	24 September - 4 November 1917
Jasta 26	11 February - 12 March 1918
Jasta 27	13 February - 14 April 1918

* This unit was created to develop a remotely controlled unmanned aircraft.

Meetkerke

This was a small village about 4 km/2.5 miles north-west of Bruges.

Units	Period of occupation
Jasta 20	June - 31 August 1917

Menin

There were three airfields around Menin, the oldest of which was Coucou (C), the second was on the east side of the town – Halluin or Menin-Ost (H), and the last, on the north side (N), was built during the Battle of Kemmel.

Units	Period of occupation
FFA (A) 204	12 March 1918 - end of occupation
FFA (A) 240	Mid-May - June 1918 (N)
FFA (A) 250	November 1916 - May 1917 (C)
Jasta 18	November 1916 - 16 June 1917 (H)
Jasta 20	6 June 1918 - end of occupation
Jasta 40	24 August - 28 September 1918 (H)
	8 October 1918 - end of occupation (H)
Jasta 51	1 October 1918 - end of occupation

Moorsele

Units	Period of occupation
FA 33	Until 25 November 1917
Schusta 26	August - 25 November 1917
FA (A) 233	12 April – end of May 1918

Oostcamp

This village south of Bruges had two aerodromes – the first just outside the village to the north and the second to the east, about 2 km/1.2 miles from Oostcamp itself.

Units	Period of occupation
FA (A) 227	end May 1917 - early 1918
Schusta 26	circa June 1917 - February/ March 1918
Schusta 21	circa August 1917 - beginning 1918
FA (A) 233	24 August - 15 November 1917
Schusta 27 B	5 November - end November 1917
Jasta 12	5 November - 16 November 1917
Jasta 17	6 November - 20 November 1917
FA (A) 258	7 November - 15 November 1917
FA (A) 211	6 December 1917 - 9 March 1918

Rumbeke Ost

During spring 1917 Rumbeke (near Roulers) got a second airfield.

Units	Period of occupation
Jasta 8	12 September 1916 - 30 September 1917
Jasta 37	20 June - 5 August 1917
Jasta 3	20 July - 17 September 1917
	20 September - 17 October 1917
Jasta 2	10 October - 13 November 1917
Jasta 7	1 March - 29 March 1918
Jasta 20	9 April - 6 June 1918
Jasta 54	4 May - 6 June 1918
Jasta 56	5 May - 30 September 1918
Jasta 50	6 June - 30 September 1918

Torhout

This small town was in the centre of the Belgian province of Western Flanders.

Units	Period of occupation
Flieger-Abteilung 48	Mid-July - mid-October 1917
Flieger-Abteilung 40	Summer - 24 August 1917
Jasta 29	1 August - 14 September 1917
Flieger-Abteilung (A) 211	10 October - 6 December 1917
Schusta 26	14 October - end November 1917

An aerial view of Rumbeke airfield, winter 1918, showing the nine tents and three aircraft (Collection Maertens).

DFW (Deutsche Flugzeugwerke) CV (No 8489/16) outside camouflaged tented hangar at Torhout airfield (own collection).

Vlisseghem

This small village was midway between Ostend and Bruges and about 4 km/2.5 miles from the coast.

Units	Period of occupation
Marine Schusta I	June - 23 September 1917
1 Marinefeldflieger-Abteilung	16 June 1917- spring 1918

Winghene

This village was 10 km/6 miles east of Torhout. Germany's second-highest-scoring ace, Ernst Udet with Jasta 37 was based here for about five months, during which time it is said that he had an affair with a local beauty.

Units	Period of occupation
FA 256	24 August 1917- end March 1918
Schusta 4	24 August - 25 November 1917
Schusta 12	18 September – mid-October 1917
Jasta 37	10 October 1917- 5 February 1918
Jasta 3	17 October 1917- 13 March 1918
FA 32	27 October - 15 November 1917
Jasta 51	January 1918
Jasta 40	10 October - 22 October 1918

The End

By the end of July 1918 German resistance was fading – the troops were exhausted, their morale was low and they lacked reserves of personnel and equipment. The Allies, on the other hand, had brought their divisions up to full strength and were concentrating on the final assault.

The Allies launched their major offensive in September 1918. On the left wing of the Western Front, Army Group Flanders, comprising the Belgian Army, some French army corps and the British Second Army – mounted the attack towards the first main objective – Ghent.

The German Fourth Army's aerial strength was dwarfed by that of Army Group Flanders. The number of Allied single-seater fighters alone was greater than the total aircraft available to the Fourth Army, which by the end of September had some 30 units: Jagdgruppe 9 (Jastas 7, 16, 20, 40, 51 and 56), Marine Jagdgeschwader, FAs 3, 6, 13, 48, (A) 204, 250, 288, RBZ 2, I and II MFFA, Schlastas 9, 16, 24 and 25, I and II Marineschlasta, BG 3 and RFA 501.

All these units were short of aircraft, and with the exception of two of the Jastas, the

rest could barely raise 60 per cent of their normal strength.

Overwhelmed by the Allies' superior strength the German High Command lost sight of the enemy advance. Despite heavy fighting and the danger of mid-air collisions with artillery shells, reconnaissance crews made courageous sorties to keep headquarters informed. In the late afternoon of 28 September Jasta 40 based at Bisseghem had to escort such a contact patrol made by a crew of FA (A) 250. Carl Degelow, CO of Jasta 40, reported:

As there was still no clear idea of the situation at the front, a very experienced infantry-support flyer was brought in to report on the English advance. Just as we formed up over our own airfield, the two-seater arrived and identified

Gotha GV of the crew Radke-Genth (see RG on fuselage, Bosta 13 of BG III) in a uncomfortable position. At the end of the war the Bostas bombed the advancing allied troops. For instance on 30 October that crew attacked the RAF at Bisseghem airfield.

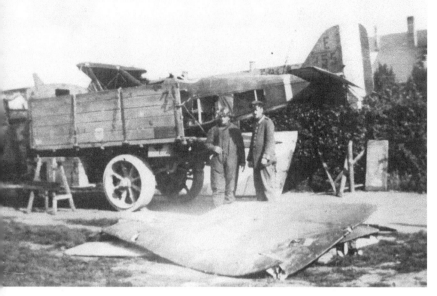

Another victim of the German pilots: on 8 August 1918, Second Lieutenant M Tison of 29 Squadron RAF was shot down at 9.10 am while attacking two German biplanes over Warneton. He was taken POW and his aircraft, a Royal Aircraft Factory SE5, No E1255, was brought to Heule airfield (Collection Raven).

itself by firing off a red flare. We immediately surrounded him on all sides and headed for the front. The observer communicated with the ground forces by flashing a light, and they responded by spreading white cloth strips to mark their positions. Our two-seater criss-crossed the front repeatedly and we could clearly see him making notes in his cockpit.

Then a swarm of 12 Englishmen attacked us. Like a wedge, our tightly led group dived on the Tommies in their loose formation, and they were unable to get to our reconnaissance plane. After a successful fight, I fired off a flare to signal for my companions to regroup.

On the ground German troops continued to put up tough resistance and on 4 October the Allies had to halt their advance. Prior to this, between 28 September and 4 October, the 11 Jastas fought a desperate battle against some 30 Allied fighter units and claimed 89 wins for only five losses. One of these was Oberleutnant Hans Gandert, commander of Jagdgruppe 9, who was shot down above Langemark on 29 September, crash-landed and was made prisoner.

Intense aerial activity continued, and the German air force suffered heavy casualties, losing 12 aircraft – seven per cent of its total strength – between 3 and 10 October,

during which period BG 3 dropped 37,500 kg/82,500 lb of bombs on Allied positions.

The German planes now worked in large formations as in this report by Belgian fighter pilot attests:

14 October 1918. 6.45 to 8.00 am, we twice attacked a group of seven Halberstadts. They had probably been attacking our troops north of Hooglede. At 12.45 am we were attacked by 30 Fokkers.

On 14 October Allied forces broke through the German defensive lines. One by one they captured the airfields and landing

strips, forcing the German squadrons to withdraw to airfields deeper into their own territory. On 16 October the naval units transferred to an airfield near Eeklo, but only two days later they had to move to Stekene, halfway along the Ghent-Antwerp road. Jastas 3, 8, 14, 54 and FA 3, 13 and (A) 203 retreated to the area around Zottegem while Jastas 7, 16, 20, 36, 51 and FA (A) 250 and 256 moved to the Ronse area. Schlastas 9, 16, 24 and 25 arrived near Oudenaarde on 7 October, where they stayed for just 16 days. The seaplanes of Ostend and Zeebruges had already left Belgium at the start of October, and on 22 October AFP 4 moved from Ghent to Antwerp.

During the last combats Leutnant Jacobs (Jasta 7), Leutnant Degelow (Js 40) Vizeflugmeister Zenses (II Marine Jasta), Leutnant Plauth (Js 20 and CO of Js 51) and Flugmeister Scharon (II Marine Jasta) were the top scorers, downing 55 Allied aircraft between 28 September and 11 November. But on 11 November 1918 the war was over. The Germans agreed to an immediate surrender and four years of war came to an end.

Today, in the many Flanders military cemeteries, both English and German, one can see the graves of some 600 members of the German air force.

Selected Bibliograpy

Archives and libraries

- Bayerisches Hauptstaatsarchiv - Kriegsarchiv – Munich
- Brussels Air Museum
- Bundesarchiv (Koblenz)
- Bundesarchiv - Militärarchiv (MAF, Freiburg im Breisgau)
- Central Library of Defence (Belgian Army - Evere)
- Center Caenepeel (Ypres)
- Center for Historical Documentation of the Belgian Armed Forces (CHDK, Evere)
- Hauptstaatsarchiv Stuttgart
- Imperial War Museum (London)
- Public Records Office (Kew, London)
- Royal Museum of Army and Military History (Brussels)
- Service Historique de la Défense (Vincennes, Paris)
- University of Texas at Dallas (History of Aviation Collection)

Books and periodicals:

- D-S ABBOTT and R DUIVEN Schlachtflieger!: Germany and the Origins of Air/Ground support, 1916-1918. Lancaster 2006
- J ANGOLLA and C HACKNEY The PLM's and Germany's First Aces. Texas 1984
- D BAKER Manfred von Richthofen. The Man and the Aircraft he flew. London 1990
- Bayerische Flieger im Weltkrieg. München 1919
- K BODENSCHATZ Jagd in Flanderns Himmel. Munich 1935
- H BORDEAUX Vie héroique de Guynemer. Paris 1925
- J BUCKLER Malaula. Der Schlachtruf meiner Staffel. Berlin 1939
- C COLE R.F.C.-Communiqués 1915-1916. London 1990
- ID RAF-Communiqués 1918. London 1990
- CROSS AND COCKADE - journal. The society of WW I Aero Historians (USA)
- CROSS AND COCKADE INTERNATIONAL - journal. The first World War Aviation Historical Society
- B. DENECKERE Luchtoorlog boven West-Vlaanderen, 1914-1918. Courtrai 1998
- B. DENECKERE Luchtoorlog boven België. 1914. Van Antwerpen tot de Zee. Roulers 2010
- R DUIVEN List of Jagdstaffeln. Unpublished study
- W von EBERHARDT Unsere Lufstreitkräfte 1914-1918. Berlin 1930
- C ELLIS History of Combat Aircraft. s.l. 1979
- E FERKO Fliegertruppe 1914-1918. Salem 1980
- ID Fliegertruppe 1914-1918 Nr. 2. Salem 1987
- A FLIPTS, M and R FAILLIE Marke II. Courtrai Marke 1984
- N L R FRANKS, F W BAILEY and R GUEST Above the Lines. The Aces and Fighter Units of the German Air Service, Naval Air Service and Flanders Marine Corps. London 1993
- N L R FRANKS, F W BAILEY and R DUIVEN The Jasta pilots. London 1996
- N L R FRANKS, H GIBLIN and N McCERY Under the Guns of the red Baron. London. 1998
- A D FUNK Unsere Luftwaffe. Jahrbuch der Luftfahrtdienst. s.l 1917
- P GAEBLER Das Marinekorps im Weltkrieg 14-18. Berlin s.d
- J GESQUIERE Furnes tijdens de Wereldoorlog 1914-1918. Bruges 1979
- P GREY and O THETFORD German Aircraft of the First World War. London 1962
- von HOEPPNER Deutschlands Krieg in der Luft. Leipzig 1921
- Im Flugzeuge gegen England und andere Flieger Geschichte. Leipzig 1915
- A IMRIE German Bombers of World War One. London 1990
- ID German Naval Air Service. London 1989
- ID German Fighter Units 1914-May 1917. London 1978
- ID German Fighter Units June 1917-1918. London 1978
- ID Pictorial History of the German Army Air Service 1914-1918. London 1971

- D JACOBSEN Trutzig und Treue. Berlin-Leipzig 1935
- P KILDUFF Germany's first Air Force 1914-1918. London 1991
- A KOCH Die Flieger-Abteilung (A) 221. Berlin 1925
- D von KORB Feldflieger an der Front. Leipzig 1916
- Die Kriegsführung im Sommer und Herbst 1917. Die Ergebnisse ausserhalb der Westfront bis 1918. Berlin 1942
- W von LANGSDORFF Kriegserlebnisse deutscher Flieger. Gütersloh 1934
- E von LOEWENSTEIN Der Frontflieger. Berlin 1937
- E LEYSE Het Belgische militaire vliegwezen tijdens de Eerste Wereldoorlog. s.l. 1978
- Der Luftkrieg 14-15. Unter Verwendung von Feldpostbriefen. Leipzig 1915
- F K MASON Battle over Britain. A History of the German Air Assaults on Great Britain. New York 1969
- Mobilmachung, Aufmarsch und erster Einsatz der deutschen Luftstreitkräfte im August 1914. Berlin 1939
- J H MORROW German Air Power in World War I. London 1982
- J MORTANE Histoire illustrée de la guerre aérienne 2 dlen
- O von MOSER Die Württemberger im Weltkriege. Stuttgart 1938
- K MUNSON Vliegtuigen uit de Eerste Wereldoorlog. Amsterdam 1969
- ID Fighters, attack and training aircraft. Poole, 1975
- Naamstenen. Brugge 1988
- G P NEUMANN. Die deutsche Luftstreitkräfte im Weltkriege. Berlin 1920
- ID In der Luft unbesiegt. Berlin
- H NOWARRA 50 Jahre Deutsche Luftwaffe 1910-1960. Deel I. Pictoral History of the Luftwaffe 1910-1915. s.l. 1964
- ID 50 Jahre Deutsche Luftwaffe 1910-1960. Deel II. Pictorial History of the Luftwaffe 1916-1917. s.l. 1964
- ID 50 Jahre Deutsche Luftwaffe 1910-1960. Deel III. Pictorial History of the Luftwaffe 1918. s.l. 1968
- ID Eisernes Kreuz und Balkenkreuz. Die Markierungen der deutschen Flugzeuge 1914-1918. Mainz 1968
- H NOWARRA and K S BROWN Von Richthofen and the Flying Circus. s.l. 1958
- N W O'CONNOR Aviation Awards of Imperial Germany in World War I, and the men who earned them. Deel I. The Aviation Awards of the Kingdom of Bavaria. Princeton 1988
- ID Aviation Awards of Imperial Germany in World War I, and the men who earned them. Deel II. The Aviation Awards of the Kingdom of Prussia. Princeton 1990
- ID Aviation Awards of Imperial Germany in World War I, and the men who earned them. Deel IV. The Aviation Awards of the Kingdom of Württemberg. Princeton 1995
- T OSTERKAMP Du oder Ich. Berlin, s.d
- Over the Front. Journal of the World War One Aviation Historians. USA
  P O Box 2475
  Rockford, IL 61132-2475, USA
- L PACKO Jabbeke 1914-1918. Aartrijke 1990
- W PIETERS Above Flanders' Fields: A Complete Record of the Belgian Fighter Pilots and Their Units During the Great War, 1914-1918. London, 1998
- A PERNET Les avions de la guerre 1914-1918. Verviers 1961
- WWI – journal PROPPELLERBLATT. Mitteilungsblatt der Interessengemeinschaft Luftfahrt 1900-1920
- W RALEIGH and H A JONES The War in the Air. Dl. I - V. London, s.d.
- M von RICHTHOFEN Der rote Kampfflieger. Berlin 1917
- J RYHEUL Marinekorps Flandern 1914-1918. Aartrijke 1996
- B SAMSON Fights and Flights. London 1930
- A SERVAIS Filations des Unités de la Force Aérienne. s.l. 1918
- P SIMKINS Air Fighting 1914-1918. The Struggle for the Air Superiority over the Western Front. London 1978
- L SLOSSE War Diary of Rumbeke 1914-1918. Bruges 1962
- T C TRADWELL and A C WOOD German Knights of the Air. New York. 1998
- E UDET Ein Fliegerleben. Berlin 1954
- E VANACKERE Von Flugplatz tot Airport, de geschiedenis van het vliegveld Wevelghem-Bisseghem 1916-1990. Courtrai 1991
- L VANOVERBEKE Moorsele, een dorp - twee vliegvelden. Courtrai 1993
- Der Weltkrieg 1914 bis 1918. Dl. V. Berlin 1929
- N WELTOBORSKY Die Flieger-Abteilung (A) 211 im Weltkriege. Zuelenroda 1938

German airfields in the province of Western Flanders (1917-1918)

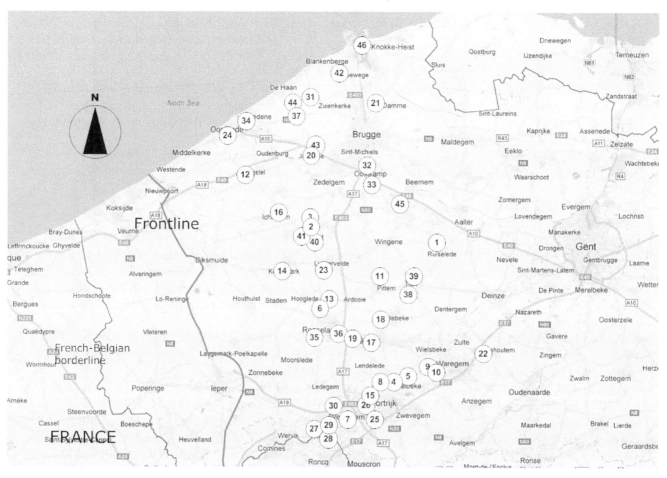

1. Aalter (Doomkerke)	17. Ingelmunster	33. Oostcamp (Erkegem)
2. Aartrijke	18. Ingelmunster (Meulebeke)	34. Ostend
3. Aartrijke (Sparappelhoek)	19. Iseghem	35. Rumbeke
4. Bavikhove	20. Jabbeke	36. Rumbeke Ost
5. Bavikhove	21. Koolkerke	37. Stalhille
6. Beveren	22. Kruishoutem	38. Thielt
7. Bisseghem	23. Lichtervelde	39. Thielt
8. Cuerne	24. Mariakerke	40. Torhout
9. Desselgem (Ooigem)	25. Marke	41. Torhout
10. Desselgem (Dries)	26. Markebeke	42. Uitkerke
11. Egem	27. Menin (Coucou)	43. Varsenare
12. Ghistelles	28. Menin (Halluin / Ost)	44. Vlisseghem
13. Ghits	29. Menin (Nord)	45. Wingene
14. Handzame	30. Moorsele	46. Zeebruges
15. Heule	31. Nieuwmunster / Houthave	
16. Ichtegem (Engel)	32. Oostcamp	

ND - #0186 - 270225 - C0 - 270/210/8 [10] - CB - 9781908487308 - Gloss Lamination